Beginning the Journey

The

Luciferian

Strategy

By

Mary Ann Levy

Foreword by Rev. Dr. Mosy U. Madugba

Luciferian Strategy

All scripture references from KJV King James Version, NIV New International Version or ASV American Standard Version

ISBN: 978-8058-76-0

Published in the Federal Republic of Nigeria by Spiritual Life Outreach Inc. a multinational Christian evangelistic/missionary organization working in several countries in Africa and some part of the world to bring the gospel to the unreached people – groups and mobilizing prayer efforts.

N/B

Bold, parenthesis or <u>underline </u>emphasis throughout the work is mine. I prefer, when reading new information, to see the "footnotes" information included in the body of the work, therefore for most of this work, that is the format I have used.

All Trade Orders To:
Goodies Supermarket and Bookshop, No 312 NTA, Road
 Mgbuoba Port Harcourt, Rivers State Nigeria
Tel: +234(0) 09060696986

Email: levybook@yahoo.com

Printed in the Federal Republic of Nigeria.**90**

ACKNOWLEDGEMENTS

Where would I be without Richard, my husband of fifty-five years! I shudder to think! He's been the wall of protection about me since the Lord brought us together on a Greyhound bus fifty-seven years ago - THAT'S another story! He's been a stalwart encouragement and my singular cheerleader from day one – I am SO thankful to our Lord for all he is to myself and our three children, who are stable and successful voices of encouragement, and our nine grandchildren, who see him as the stable man of integrity he is and now our six – so far – great-grandchildren.

And I could not continue without thanking our dear friends Al and Saundra Reed, who have been solid voices of encouragement through our forty years of friendship and who gave me much needed correction and suggestions during this project. And our dear friend Janice Arnoldy, who has the unique ability to see without judgment, so that even when I would try to bring judgment against myself by questioning myself through the lens of someone's opinion against me, she always manages to point out the truth separated from the judgment – amazing Gift to us and the Body of Christ!

And, of course our dear friends and brother and sister and Apostles and mentors, Mosy and Gloria Madugba. When I think I'm just doing "what was my duty to do" they reflect it back to me as a precious gift – which in turn becomes a precious gift to me. Their humility is astounding, considering the *power* of the Gospel they walk in! They are true Apostles, whose lives are parallel to those we read of in the Word. In the years we have been walking together I have seen them speak a word in season to a battered Saint and watch that person *become* – what a blessing to see so many come into their calling and purpose through a right word spoken in season with Apostolic Authority! But to have that same experience myself came as a sudden surprise when I showed them notes Holy Spirit had had me put together for a "teaching". Richard and I pondered *where* to share the notes or *what* to do with them! Then Mosy and Gloria came to stay with us and Holy Spirit reminded me of the teaching notes – I shared them - and the next day received the commanded blessing, "You MUST write a book!" stunned, I responded, "Then you must pray for me to be able to do that!" That night, contemplating what *would* I say, I wrote the Introduction! Such is the power of Apostolic Grace! Their prayers, encouragement and consistent love have brought us through many of life's trials and joys, and we thank the Lord abundantly for the gift of them in our lives.

TABLE OF CONTENT
INTRODUCTION

NEW BEGINNINGS

Foreword

Every Christian must read this book. Ignorance is a big deal. It is a limiting incapacitating expensive disease. Satan offered to help Ms Eve in Garden of Eden to solve this problem and she lost control of her mind and went for it from the wrong and evil source. If you are ignorant, you are at the mercy of anybody who claims he knows more than you. You live with inferiority complex.

Even now, ignorance is the reason why many live in mental, psychological, emotional, social, political and spiritual bondage. It is a debilitating and terrible disease.

Church folks are not left out from this malaise. All sorts of things go on in different parts of planet earth in the name of spiritual warfare and casting out devils from people and locations. If only they have adequate relevant knowledge, they would have been doing better.

In 1Cor.9:26, St. Paul wrote giving a good assessment of his ministry impact " *So I fight not as one who "beats" empty air."* He knocked out his foes.

Towards the tail end of his ministry on earth, he wrote giving a conclusive assessment of the victorious way he has served God and wrote in 2 Timothy 4:7 *"I have fought a good fight."* As a veteran, he wrote to advise me and you in1Timothy 6:12 to *"Fight the good fight of faith, lay hold on eternal life."* My brother, my sister, read on, conquer your mental laziness and preconceived biases and raise the tempo with which you approach the enemy as a frontline combat soldier with adequate historical knowledge of the spiritual terrain where we fight.

One of his success secrets was knowledge of relevant spiritual information and revelations. He personally had several spiritual encounters and was open to learn what he did not know.

It's our turn today to make similar or greater impact. In your palms is a book full of rare but helpful information for your future spiritual combat battles on earth.

I have known Mary Ann Levy for close to 30 years. She has gone through all our training sessions in Spiritual Warfare and related courses. Together with her husband, Elder Richard Levy, they now teach others all over America on these subjects. She is outstandingly passionate for God and His Kingdom. She took time to research into what she brings to us. Enjoy a well prepared 'dish' for you and may the knowledge you gain from it make you a more effective and impactful prayer warrior and spiritual combat soldier in Jesus' name, Amen!

Dr. Mosy U. Madugba
International Head Coordinator, Ministers Prayer Network.
A professor of Missions and Biblical Theology. A global advocate of the 5th Great Awakening-A prolonged unprecedented season of heaven-sent revival.
Nov.13, 2017

INTRODUCTION

We have all heard the stories and seen the sidelong glances directed toward those who believe in "Conspiracy Theories". Many times they are pictured as wearing tin-foil hats. In Christian circles, those who believe there is a "behind the scenes agenda" directing the affairs of the earth are often accused of, "looking for a demon under every bush."

Well, the fact of the matter is, there *are* Conspiracies abounding, and the Bible helps us uncover many of them, if we know where to look. Lucifer has, from day one, conspired to steal Creation from our Creator God, and if he's not able to steal it, then he'll be satisfied to corrupt it. This work will follow that trail of conspiracies down through the ages until now, and unfold and expose some of his plots against us, mankind, God's final and ultimate Creation. In uncovering and exposing the strategies against us and Creation, we understand and are better prepared to cooperate with the Father's strategies. Scripture exhorts us in

II Corinthians 2:11

> *...in order that Satan might not outwit us. For we are not unaware of his schemes.*

It is *past* time for the Sons of God to be made manifest in the earth!

In the Bible we're told of Lucifer's response to God's ultimate Creation:

How art thou fallen from heaven, O Lucifer, son of the morning! how art thou cut down to the ground, which didst weaken the nations! For thou hast said in thine heart, I will ascend into heaven, I will exalt my throne above the stars of God: I will sit also upon the mount of the congregation, in the sides of the north: I will ascend above the heights of the clouds; I will be like the most High. Isaiah 14:12-14 (KJV)

In doing so he was ejected from heaven.

In our looking at the beginning and following his trail throughout history, we're going to look at many reference materials and sources of information. When my husband and I were first discovering this history and beginning to understand *why* it was important for us to have this information *today*, we were introduced to books such as the Books of Jasher and Enoch, and we were skeptical. Were these reliable sources? In our search and research, we found many validating sources and will share them in this work.

God told Daniel:
"But as for you, Daniel, conceal these words and seal up the   book until the end of time; many will go back and forth, and knowledge will increase." (Daniel 12:4 NAS)

Knowledge is greatly increasing in our day in all areas. The Lord is breaking open His Word almost daily with new Revelation and understanding. Science is unfolding ancient "secrets" with the discovery of such things as DNA. All of this helps those of us with the will and purpose to follow the threads of truth and thereby discover what the Lord has known all along - the strategies of Lucifer to corrupt Creation and mankind. In that discovery, we find the strategies of Lucifer, and in finding these strategies we learn of the Fathers counterattack!

Let's enjoy the journey!

Chapter 1

BEGINNING THE JOURNEY

As we walk through this historical journey, we will establish the authority and veracity of Biblical as well as various extra-biblical references to the Fallen Angels and their offspring, the Giants and the Nephilim.

The purpose of this work is to *know* the strategies of our enemy so that we can *effectively* counter those strategies in the earth. In *"The Art of War"* by Sun Tzu, a reference book used in War Colleges, we are wisely advised:

> *If you know the enemy and know yourself, you need not fear the result of a hundred battles. If you know yourself but not the enemy, for every victory gained you will also suffer a defeat. If you know neither the enemy nor yourself, you will succumb in every battle.*

Essential knowledge is vital for victorious Christian living. This is one of the purposes of this work. This book will help us to learn the strategies of our enemy, so that we will not be caught unaware of his schemes.

In Luke 19:13 Jesus tells a parable, in it he exhorts us to "*occupy until I return*". That word "occupy" doesn't mean to just take up space in a church pew or comfy chair until we're raptured out one day!

The Strong's Greek definition "occupy" is to "fulfill". from <G303> (ana) and <G4137> (pleroo); to complete; by implication to occupy, supply; figurative to accomplish (by coincidence or obedience) :- fill up, fulfil, occupy, supply.

Part of the wonderful prayer of Jesus in the book of John 17:15 (KJV)was:

> *I pray not that thou shouldest take them out of the world, but that thou shouldest keep them from the evil one.*

Also in John 17:17-18 (KJV)

> *He said "Sanctify them through thy truth: thy word is truth. As thou hast sent me into the world, even so have I also sent them into the world.*

Jesus knew He was leaving evil in the world, but He prayed we would be kept from that evil. In the ninth chapter of Luke, Jesus begins by telling His disciples:

> *Luke 9:1 (KJV)*
> *Then he called his twelve disciples together, and gave them power and authority over all devils, and to cure diseases.*

He gave us *all* power *and* Authority over *all* devils *and* to cure diseases, it's *past* time we begin to function in the Authority we were given as sons of God! Luke confirms this in the tenth chapter verse nineteen:

Luke 10:19 (KJV)
*Behold, I give unto you power to tread on serpents and scorpions, and over **all** the power of the enemy: and **nothing** shall by any means hurt you.*
(emphasis mine)

An important point to remember is the last part of this verse:

Luke 10:19-20 (KJV)
*Notwithstanding, in this **rejoice not**, that the spirits are subject unto you; but rather rejoice, because your names are written in heaven.* **(emphasis mine)**

Rejoicing that our names are written in the Lambs' Book of Life rather than the fact we have authority over the enemy is a topic for another book, but an important foundational key to remember as we go through life.

As we grow in our understanding of Who we are in Him and Who He is in us, and we experience victories in overcoming our common enemy, there can be a temptation to want to bully the enemy, to exalt in our victories by resorting to childish ways and taunting the enemy. We never taunt the enemy, in doing so you are taking on his ways and his nature rather than that of our Father and King.

Now, the question is: Why did Jesus give us this Power and Authority? How are we to function as "Ambassadors" of His Kingdom?

> II Corinthians 5: *19 states God was reconciling the world to* Himself in Christ, not *counting men's trespasses against them. And He has committed to us the message of reconciliation. Therefore we are ambassadors for Christ, as though God were making His appeal through us. We implore you on behalf of Christ: Be reconciled to God.*

Historically, the only interpretation of this scripture is that we are sent into the world to share the Gospel with mankind. However, if we look at the word "world" in this and other scriptures, we find the Greek word is "kosmos" our "cosmos," which speaks of all of creation. We, His Ambassadors are to bring His Kingdom into all of creation. Romans 8: 19-22 tells us "creation is groaning for the revelation of the Sons of God."

> *For the creation waits in eager expectation for the children of God to be revealed. For the creation was subjected to frustration, not by its own choice, but by the will of the one who subjected it, in hope that the creation itself will be liberated from its bondage to decay and brought into the freedom and glory of the children of God. We know that the whole creation has been groaning as in the pains of childbirth right up to the present time.*

So, we are commissioned to not only bring the message of Redemption to mankind but also to all of Creation. In order for us to fulfill this Commission effectively, we need to discover the sin foundation to address. Just as when we bring the message of Salvation to an individual or group, we address the foundational sin and lead them to repentance and reconciliation to the Father.

In dealing with Creation, we follow the same principle, we search the history to discover where Creation has been captured, enslaved or in some way brought into the captivity of the enemy and we address

those foundations. We, as the Sons of God, bring repentance on behalf of Creation for its' having been made a slave of sin, we call on it to align itself with the Living Word of God. We remind the heavens it was created to declare the Glory of the Lord and the earth was created to bring forth Truth and Righteousness. The following scriptures are relevant to this truth.

Psalm 19:1
The heavens are telling of the glory of God; And their expanse is declaring the work of His hands.
Psalm 50:6
And the heavens declare His righteousness, For God Himself is judge.
Psalm 89:5
The heavens will praise Your wonders, O LORD; Your faithfulness also in the assembly of the holy ones.
Psalm 97:6
The heavens declare His righteousness, And all the peoples have seen His glory.
Psalm 145:10
All Your works shall give thanks to You, O LORD, And Your godly ones shall bless You.
Psalm 85:11
Truth shall spring out of the earth; and righteousness shall look down from heaven.

Which brings us to the purpose of this work. In our searching through history to discovered how to set Creation free, we discover not only the iniquity Creation has been corrupted with, but we discovered the Luciferian strategy in his step-by-step attempt to ensnare *all* of God's creation.

The Luciferian Strategy

Chapter 2

LUCIFER'S ORIGINS

In the beginning, according to scripture, Lucifer was of the highest rank of Angelic beings. Below are just very few of the scriptures referring to the Cherubim. They certainly are *not* the chubby, little children the enemy would like us to think they are! *Isaiah 14:12-15 states this clearly;*

> *How you have fallen from heaven, morning star, son of the dawn! You have been cast down to the earth, you who once laid low the nations! You said in your heart, "I will ascend to the heavens; I will raise my throne above the stars of God; I will sit enthroned on the mount of assembly, on the utmost heights of Mount Zaphon. I will ascend above the tops of the clouds; I will make myself like the Most High." But you are brought down to the realm of the dead, to the depths of the pit.*

Ezekiel 28:14 also states
You were the anointed cherub who covers, *And I placed you there You were on the holy mountain of God; You walked in the midst of the stones of fire.* **(emphasis mine)**

Genesis 3:24 (KJV)

> *So he drove out the man; and he placed at the east of the garden of Eden Cherubims, and a flaming sword which turned every way, to keep the way of the tree of life.*

2 Samuel 22:6-11 (KJV)

> *The sorrows of hell compassed me about; the snares of death prevented me; In my distress I called upon the LORD, and cried to my God: and he did hear my voice out of his temple, and my cry did enter into his ears. Then the earth shook and trembled; the foundations of heaven moved and shook, because he was wroth. There went up a smoke out of his nostrils, and fire out of his mouth devoured: coals were kindled by it. He bowed the heavens also, and came down; and darkness was under his feet And he rode upon a cherub, and did fly: and he was seen upon the wings of the wind.*

Our enemy is also depicted as a snake in the Garden of Eden. "Snake" is the translation of the Hebrew "Nachash," meaning Shining One.

Now, how can he be both a "Cherub" *and* a snake? If we study more on this, we will see that a Cherub was a *rank* of Angel, just as a Captain, or Lieutenant or Sergeant would be on a Police Department or in the Army, whereas a Nachash would be a *type* of Angelic being.

So, what does a Nachash look like according to scripture? The Hebrew meaning of the word Nachash is "bright, shining one" and obviously from reading the Genesis account, he was upright. The rank of Cherub were described as a variety of beings, but the type of angel known as serpent-like or dragons are described as Seraphim.

- In the Bible, the word (sarap) is used in two different scenes. Most famous, it denotes the flying, supernatural six-winged creatures that surround God's throne in the vision of Isaiah (Isaiah 6:2). Much later, John the Revelator also sees a vision of God's throne and saw what looked like the same creatures (REVELATION 4:8). Both Isaiah and John heard these creatures cry "Holy, holy, holy".

John and Isaiah both heard these creatures crying "Holy, Holy, Holy" because obviously they are of the type of Seraph that did *not* follow Lucifer when he was thrown out of heaven.

- The masculine noun שרף (*sarap*) denotes a fiery serpent and is used five times: Numbers 21:6 and 21:8, Deuteronomy 8:15, Isaiah 14:29 and 30:6. The exact same word is used in Isaiah 6:2 to describe the angelic beings known as Seraphim.

> **Revelation 12:9 (KJV)**
> *And the great dragon was cast out, that old serpent, called the Devil, and Satan, which deceiveth the whole world: he was cast out into the earth, and his angels were cast out with him.*

In our vernacular "dragons" have taken on an evil connotation because of Satan and mythology and various fictional stories. However, if we did not have these preconceived ideas of Dragons as being evil and saw a huge being with six wings and the Glory of God coming from its' mouth as a fire we would be awestruck!

The name "Satan" or "Lucifer":
The common names of "Satan" or "Lucifer" which we call the enemy, is not his "Name" it's a Title, it's a descriptive noun – which is why we rebuke a "deaf and dumb spirit" for instance – it's not the demons *name*, rather it's descriptive of its' activity in that particular situation.
From wiki-pedia:

Hebrew Bible

> The original **Hebrew** term *satan* is a noun from a verb meaning primarily "to obstruct, oppose", as it is found in **Numbers** 22:22, **1 Samuel** 29:4, **Psalms** 109:6.[6] *Ha-Satan* is traditionally translated as "the accuser" or "the adversary". The definite article *ha-* (English: "the") is used to show that this is a title bestowed on a being, versus the name of a being. Thus, this being would be referred to as "the satan"

But for the purpose of this work, we will use the term "Lucifer," as it's more easily understandable who it is we are referring to.

So, we see that Lucifer, who was once one of the highest ranking angels in Heaven, rebelled against God and decided he would be "like" God.

In their book, *On the Path of the Immortals*, Authors Tom Horn and Chris Putnam write:

> "Hebrew Bible scholar Michael Heiser argue that the so-called "serpent" in the Garden of Eden was no snake. The noun spelled *Nachash* in Hebrew can mean "snake or serpent" or, as a verb, "to practice divination," but as an adjective, it means "bright, brazen." In Hebrew grammar, it is common for adjectives to be used. Thus, it is a valid option to translate *Nachash* as a noun meaning "shining one." Heiser concludes, "Eve was not talking to a snake. She was speaking to a bright, shining upright being who was serpentine in appearance, and who was trying to bewitch her with lies." This makes the Genesis account seem all the more plausible; after all, snakes do not have vocal chords and Eve was not immediately taken aback as one would expect, given a talking snake, suggesting that perhaps she was even accustomed to seeing such entities. It is rather satisfying to know that even in light of what we have learned from Ugaric and Egyptian texts concerning the ancient context of Scripture, the controversial Hebrew Bible passages (Genesis 2, Isaiah 14, and Ezekiel 28) classically used to describe the devil of New Testament theology (often to the disapproval of scholars) can now be rigorously reconciled.

Heiser addresses three passages as a composite sketch:
- Genesis 3: the Nachash (Shining One) is put down on the ground (denoted by the "eating dust" reference in 3:14).

- Isaiah 14: *Helel* (Shining One) is "brought down to Sheol" (v 11) "cut down to the earth" (erets) " (v 12); "thrust down to Sheol, to the recesses of the pit." (v 15).
- Ezekiel 28: The brilliant shining Cherub is "cast from the (cosmic) mountain of God" (v 16) and "cast to the ground" (erets) (v 17).

Heiser explains:

All three have a shining supernatural being in Eden who rebelled against God, who sought to usurp the headship of the divine council, who was cast from God's presence and who was placed beneath the created things he vowed to rule, sentenced to the domain of the underworld.

Genesis 3:14 (KJV)

And the LORD God said unto the serpent, Because thou hast done this, thou art cursed above all cattle, and above every beast of the field; upon thy belly shalt thou go, and dust – from [3] <H6080> (`aphar); dust (as powdered or gray); hence clay, earth, mud :- ashes, dust, earth, ground, morter, powder, rubbish - shalt thou eat all the days of thy life:

It would appear from the study of this scripture that The Creator God demoted Lucifer, a Cherub of the Highest Order, who was created a Nachash or Serpent-like dragon-looking creature, who at one time breathed the Fire of God's Glory. This Being, because of his corruption of creation, was demoted to a crawling serpent-like creature, stripped of all Glory, and bound to "eat dust," the dust of the earth, until the end of days.

The Authors of *On the Path of the Immortals,* Tom Horn and Chris Putnam go on to say:

> We believe that the time draws near when the final aspect of Satan's sentence will be executed and all hell will break loose on earth when the portal to the abyss is opened.

Chapter 3

AFTER LUCIFER'S FALL

Apparently Lucifer did not learn from his demotion. Genesis 6: 1-13 shows his on-going attempt to destroy Creation, and if not destroy, to corrupt. It bears our looking at this scripture again in light of our study.

> And it came to pass, when men began to multiply on the face of the earth, and daughters were born unto them, That the sons of God saw the daughters of men that they were fair; and they took them wives of all which they chose. And the Lord said, My spirit shall not always strive with man, for that he also is flesh: yet his days shall be an hundred and twenty years. There were giants in the earth in those days; and also after that, when the sons of God came in unto the daughters of men, and they bare children to them, the same became mighty men which were of old, men of renown. And God saw that the wickedness of man was great in the earth, and that every imagination of the thoughts of his heart was only evil continually. And it repented the Lord that he had made man on the earth, and it grieved him at his heart. And the Lord said, I will destroy man whom I have created from the face of the earth; both man, and beast, and the creeping

thing, and the fowls of the air; for it repenteth me that I have made them. But Noah found grace in the eyes of the Lord. These are the generations of Noah: Noah was a just man and perfect in his generations, and Noah walked with God. And Noah begat three sons, Shem, Ham, and Japheth. The earth also was corrupt before God, and the earth was filled with violence. And God looked upon the earth, and, behold, it was corrupt; for all flesh had corrupted his way upon the earth. And God said unto Noah, The end of all flesh is come before me; for the earth is filled with violence through them; and, behold, I will destroy them with the earth.

It has been said, "it is impossible for Angels to have sex with women and have seed to bear children." However, if we look again at God's discourse with the serpent in the Garden, God said in Genesis 3:15 (KJV)

*And I will put enmity between thee and the woman, and between **thy seed** and her seed; it shall bruise thy head, and thou shalt bruise his heel.(**emphasis mine**)*

Therefore, it must be possible for these angelic beings to have seed. And, as they are created *eternal* beings, when their seed is mixed with the human genome there is a life force created that isn't subject to the limitations of humanity.

According to the Book of Enoch these Angelic beings were given the responsibility of watching over creation after God completed His work. So, as much as is possible in the limitations of this work, let's first establish the veracity of the Book of Enoch. There are *many* Reference works referring to the Book of Enoch, some positive, some negative, for those of you who want to do further research. For this work, it was my finding that the Book of Enoch, as well as the Book of Jasher was consistent with the whole counsel of God and the Canonical Scripture, and in fact is used by many reputable Theologians as reference.

From Wikipedia:

*The Book of Enoch (also 1 Enoch; Ge'ez: is an ancient Jewish religious work, ascribed by tradition to Enoch, the great-grandfather of Noah. There is little doubt that 1 Enoch was influential in molding New Testament doctrines about the Messiah, the Son of Man, the messianic kingdom, demonology, the resurrection, **and** eschatology. The limits of the influence of 1 Enoch are discussed at length by R.H. Charles, E Isaac, and G.W. Nickelsburg in their respective translations and commentaries. Biblical apocrypha, such as Jubilees, 2 Baruch, 2 Esdras, Apocalypse of Abraham **and** 2 Enoch, though even in these cases, the connection is typically more branches of a common trunk than direct development.*
https://en.wikipedia.org/wiki/Book_of_Enoch

Under *Aramaic*: Eleven **Aramaic**-language fragments of the Book of Enoch were found in cave 4 of Qumran in 1948[38] and are in the care of the Israel Antiquities Authority. They were translated for and discussed by Józef Milik and Matthew Black in *The Books of Enoch*.

A short section of 1 Enoch (1:9) is cited in Jude 1:14–15, and is attributed to "Enoch the Seventh from Adam"
Jude 1:14-16 (KJV)

And Enoch also, the seventh from Adam, prophesied of these, saying, Behold, the Lord cometh with ten thousands of his saints, ¹⁵ To execute judgment upon all, and to convince all that are ungodly among them of all their ungodly deeds which they have ungodly committed, and of all their hard speeches which ungodly sinners have spoken against him. ¹⁶ These are murmurers, complainers, walking after their own lusts; and their mouth speaketh great swelling words, having men's persons in admiration because of advantage.

There is much historical evidence to the veracity of the Book of Enoch as well as the Book of Jasher, I leave it to you the reader to do further research to satisfy yourself if you are still in doubt.

Book of Jasher:

In the Book of Jasher, chapter 4 verse 18 through 19, when these fallen angels came to earth, they took whatever and whomever they lusted after:

And their judges and rulers went to the daughters of men and took their wives by force from their husbands according to their choice, and the sons of men in those days took from the cattle of the earth, the beasts of the field and the fowls of the air, and taught the mixture of animals of one species with the

other, in order therewith to provoke the Lord; and God saw
the whole earth and it was corrupt, for all flesh had corrupted
its ways upon earth, all men and all animals.
19 And the Lord said, I will blot out man that I created from the
face of the earth, yea from man to the birds of the air, together
with cattle and beasts that are in the field for I repent that I
made them. http://www.sacredtexts.com/chr/apo/jasher/4.htm

Fallen Angels as recorded in the Book of Enoch:
The following chapters of the Book of Enoch give a clearer picture
of exactly what took place in the period of time recorded in Genesis
six.

Enoch Chapter 7:
1It happened after the sons of men had multiplied in those
days, that daughters were born to them, elegant and
beautiful. And when the angels, the sons of heaven, beheld
them, they became enamoured of them, saying to each other,
Come, let us select for ourselves wives from the progeny of
men, and let us beget children. Then their leader Samyaza
said to them; I fear that you may perhaps be indisposed to
the performance of this enterprise; And that I alone shall
suffer for so grievous a crime. But they answered him and
said; We all swear; And bind ourselves by mutual
execrations, that we will not change our intention, but
execute our projected undertaking. Then they swore all
together, and all bound themselves by mutual execrations.
Their whole number was two hundred, who descended upon
Ardis. That mountain therefore was called Armon, because

they had sworn upon it, and bound themselves by mutual execrations.
(Mt. Armon, or Mt. Hermon, derives its name from the Hebrew word herem, a curse.)

These are the names of their chiefs: Samyaza, who was their leader, Urakabarameel, Akibeel, Tamiel, Ramuel, Danel, Azkeel, Saraknyal, Asael, Armers, Batraal, Anane, Zavebe, Samsaveel, Ertael, Turel, Yomyael, Arazyal. These were the prefects of the two hundred angels, and the remainder were all with them. (6The Aramaic texts preserve an earlier list of names of these Watchers: Semihazah; Artqoph; Ramtel; Kokabel; Ramel; Danieal; Zeqiel; Baraqel; Asael; Hermoni; Matarel; Ananel; Stawel; Samsiel; Sahriel; Tummiel; Turiel; Yomiel; Yhaddiel). Then they took wives, each choosing for himself; whom they began to approach, and with whom they cohabited; teaching them sorcery, incantations, and the dividing of roots and trees. And the women conceiving brought forth giants, 12Whose stature was each three hundred cubits.

According to https://www.convert-me.com, three hundred Cubits equals 450 *feet*...a Giant by *any* standard! Amos 2:9 records the Lord saying:

Amos 2:9 (KJV)
 *Yet destroyed I the Amorite before them, **whose height was like the height of the cedars**, and he was strong as the oaks; yet I destroyed his fruit from above, and his roots from beneath. (**emphasis mine**)*

According to www.aboutcedartrees.com, Cedar trees are large, evergreen trees of the family *Cupressaceae*. Cedar trees will usually grow to a height of up to fifty feet, but others can reach one hundred or more feet in height.

The book of Enoch goes on to record in Chapter seven:

And all the others together with them took unto themselves wives, and each chose for himself one, and they began to go in unto them and to defile themselves with them, and they taught them charms and enchantments, and the cutting of roots, and made them acquainted with plants. And they became pregnant, and they bare great giants, whose height was three thousand ells: Who consumed all the acquisitions of men. And when men could no longer sustain them, the giants turned against them and devoured mankind. And they began to sin against birds, and beasts, and reptiles, and fish, and to devour one another's flesh, and drink the blood. Then the earth laid accusation against the lawless ones.

Enoch Chapter 8

Moreover Azazyel taught men to make swords, knives, shields, breastplates, the fabrication of mirrors, and the workmanship of bracelets and ornaments, the use of paint, the beautifying of the eyebrows, the use of stones of every valuable and select kind, and all sorts of dyes, so that the world became altered. Impiety increased; fornication multiplied; and they transgressed and corrupted all their ways. Amazarak taught all the sorcerers, and dividers of roots: Armers taught the solution of sorcery; Barkayal taught the observers of the stars,

Akibeel taught signs; Tamiel taught astronomy; And Asaradel taught the motion of the moon, And men, being destroyed, cried out; and their voice reached to heaven.

Enoch Chapter 9

Then Michael and Gabriel, Raphael, Suryal, and Uriel, looked down from heaven, and saw the quantity of blood which was shed on earth, and all the iniquity which was done upon it, and said one to another, It is the voice of their cries; the earth deprived of her children has cried even to the gate of heaven. And now to you, O you holy one of heaven, the souls of men complain, saying, Obtain Justice for us with the Most High. Then they said to their Lord, the King, You are Lord of lords, God of gods, King of kings. The throne of your glory is forever and ever, and forever and ever is your name sanctified and glorified. You are blessed and glorified. You have made all things; you possess power over all things; and all things are open and manifest before you. You behold all things, and nothing can be concealed from you. You have seen what Azazyel has done, how he has taught every species of iniquity upon earth, and has disclosed to the world all the secret things which are done in the heavens. Samyaza also has taught sorcery, to whom you have given authority over those who are associated with him. They have gone together to the daughters of men; have lain with them; have become polluted; And have discovered crimes to them.
(Discovered crimes. Or, "revealed these sins")
The women likewise have brought forth giants. Thus has the whole earth been filled with blood and with iniquity. And now behold the souls of those who are dead, cry out. And complain even to the gate of heaven. Their groaning ascends; nor can they

escape from the unrighteousness which is committed on earth.
You know all things, before they exist. You know these things,
and what has been done by them; yet you do not speak to us.
What on account of these things ought we to do to them?

Enoch Chapter 10

Then the Most High, the Great and Holy One spoke, and sent
Arsayalalyur (Here one Greek text reads "Uriel.") to the son of
Lamech,(Noah). Saying, Say to him in my name, Conceal
yourself. Then explain to him the consummation which is about
to take place; for all the earth shall perish; the waters of a deluge
shall come over the whole earth, and all things which are in it
shall be destroyed. And now teach him how he may escape, and
how his seed may remain in all the earth. Again the Lord said to
Raphael, Bind Azazyel hand and foot; cast him into darkness;
and opening the desert which is in Dudael, cast him in there.
Throw upon him hurled and pointed stones, covering him with
darkness; There shall he remain forever; cover his face, that he
may not see the light. And in the great day of judgment let him
be cast into the fire. Restore the earth, which the angels have
corrupted; and announce life to it, that I may revive it. All the
sons of men shall not perish in consequence of every secret, by
which the Watchers have destroyed, and which they have
taught, their offspring. All the earth has been corrupted by the
effects of the teaching of Azazyel. To him therefore ascribe the
whole crime. To Gabriel also the Lord said, Go to the biters,[3] to
the reprobates, to the children of fornication; and destroy the
children of fornication, the offspring of the Watchers, from
among men; bring them forth, and excite them one against
another. Let them perish by mutual slaughter; for length of days

shall not be theirs. They shall all entreat you, but their fathers shall not obtain their wishes respecting them; for they shall hope for eternal life, and that they may live, each of them, five hundred years. To Michael likewise the Lord said, Go and announce his crime to Samyaza, and to the others who are with him, who have been associated with women, that they might be polluted with all their impurity. And when all their sons shall be slain, when they shall see the perdition of their beloved, bind them for seventy generations underneath the earth, even to the day of judgment, and of consummation, until the judgment, the effect of which will last forever, be completed.

Then shall they be taken away into the lowest depths of the fire in torments; and in confinement shall they be shut up forever. Immediately after this shall he, (Samyaza) together with them, burn and perish; they shall be bound until the consummation of many generations. Destroy all the souls addicted to dalliance, and the offspring of the Watchers, for they have tyrannized over mankind. (Dalliance. Or, "lust"). Let every oppressor perish from the face of the earth; Let every evil work be destroyed; The plant of righteousness and of rectitude appear, and its produce become a blessing. Righteousness and rectitude shall be forever planted with delight. And then shall all the saints give thanks, and live until they have begotten a thousand children, while the whole period of their youth, and their Sabbaths shall be completed in peace. In those days all the earth shall be cultivated in righteousness; it shall be wholly planted with trees, and filled with benediction; every tree of delight shall be planted in it. In it shall vines be planted; and the vine which shall be planted in it shall yield fruit to satiety; every seed, which shall be sown in it, shall produce for one measure a thousand; and one measure of olives shall produce ten presses of oil. Purify the earth from all oppression, from all injustice, from all crime, from all impiety, and from all the pollution which is committed upon it. Exterminate them from the earth. Then shall all the children of men be righteous, and all nations shall pay me divine honours, and bless me; and all shall adore me. The earth shall be cleansed from all corruption, from every crime, from all punishment, and from all suffering; neither will I again send a deluge upon it from generation to generation forever. In those days I will open the treasures of blessing which are in heaven, that I may cause them to descend upon earth, and upon all the works and labour of man. Peace and equity shall associate with the sons of men all the days of the world, in every generation of it.

Enoch Chapter 12

Before all these things Enoch was concealed; nor did any one of the sons of men know where he was concealed, where he had been, and what had happened. He was wholly engaged with the holy ones, and with the Watchers in his days. I, Enoch, was blessing the great Lord and King of peace. And behold the Watchers called me Enoch the scribe. Then the Lord said to me: Enoch, scribe of righteousness, go tell the Watchers of heaven, who have deserted the lofty sky, and their holy everlasting station, who have been polluted with women. And have done as the sons of men do, by taking to themselves wives, and who have been greatly corrupted on the earth; That on the earth they shall never obtain peace and remission of sin. For they shall not rejoice in their offspring; they shall behold the slaughter of their beloved;

shall lament for the destruction of their sons; and shall petition for ever; but shall not obtain mercy and peace.

Enoch Chapter 13

Then Enoch, passing on, said to Azazyel: You shalt not obtain peace. A great sentence is gone forth against you. He shall bind you; Neither shall relief, mercy, and supplication be yours, on account of the oppression which you have taught; which you have discovered to the children of men. And on account of every act of blasphemy, tyranny, and sin, which you have discovered to the children of men. Then departing from him I spoke to them all together; And they all became terrified, and trembled; 6Beseeching me to write for them a memorial of supplication, that they might obtain forgiveness; and that I might make the memorial of their prayer ascend up before the God of heaven; because they could not themselves thenceforwards address him, nor raise up their eyes to heaven on account of the disgraceful offence for which they were judged. Then I wrote a memorial of their prayer and supplication, for their spirits, for everything which they had done, and for the subject of their entreaty, that they might obtain remission and rest. Proceeding on, I continued over the waters of Danbadan, which is on the right to the west of Armon, reading the memorial of their prayer, until I fell asleep. And behold a dream came to me, and visions appeared above me. I fell down and saw a vision of punishment, that I might relate it to the sons of heaven, and reprove them. When I awoke I went to them. All being collected together stood weeping in Oubelseyael, which is situated between Libanos and Seneser, with their faces veiled. I related in their presence all the visions which I had seen, and my dream;

And began to utter these words of righteousness, reproving the Watchers of heaven.

Enoch Chapter 14

This is the book of the words of righteousness, and of the reproof of the Watchers, who belong to the world, according to that which He, who is holy and great, commanded in the vision. I perceived in my dream, that I was now speaking with a tongue of flesh, and with my breath, which the Mighty One has put into the mouth of men, that they might converse with it. And understand with the heart. As he has created and given to men the power of comprehending the word of understanding, so has he created and given to me the power of reproving the Watchers, the offspring of heaven. I have written your petition; and in my vision it has been shown me, that what you request will not be granted you as long as the world endures. Judgment has been passed upon you: your request will not be granted you. From this time forward, never shall you ascend into heaven; He has said, that on the earth He will bind you, as long as the world endures. But before these things you shall behold the destruction of your beloved sons; you shall not possess them, but they shall fall before you by the sword. Neither shall you entreat for them, nor for yourselves; But you shall weep and supplicate in silence. The words of the book which I wrote. A vision thus appeared to me. Behold, in that vision clouds and a mist invited me; agitated stars and flashes of lightning impelled and pressed me forwards, while winds in the vision assisted my flight, accelerating my progress. They elevated me aloft to heaven. I proceeded, until I arrived at a wall built with stones of crystal. A vibrating flame surrounded it, which began to strike me with terror. Into this vibrating flame

I entered; And drew nigh to a spacious habitation built also with stones of crystal. Its walls too, as well as pavement, were formed with stones of crystal, and crystal likewise was the ground. Its roof had the appearance of agitated stars and flashes of lightning; and among them were cherubim of fire in a stormy sky.A flame burned around its walls; and its portal blazed with fire. When I entered into this dwelling, it was hot as fire and cold as ice. No trace of delight or of life was there. Terror overwhelmed me, and a fearful shaking seized me. Violently agitated and trembling, I fell upon my face. In the vision I looked, And behold there was another habitation more spacious than the former, every entrance to which was open before me, erected in the midst of a vibrating flame. So greatly did it excel in all points, in glory, in magnificence, and in magnitude, that it is impossible to describe to you either the splendour or the extent of it. Its floor was on fire; above were lightnings and agitated stars, while its roof exhibited a blazing fire. Attentively I surveyed it, and saw that it contained an exalted throne; The appearance of which was like that of frost; while its circumference resembled the orb of the brilliant sun; and there was the voice of the cherubim. From underneath this mighty throne rivers of flaming fire issued. To look upon it was impossible. One great in glory sat upon it: Whose robe was brighter than the sun, and whiter than snow. No angel was capable of penetrating to view the face of Him, the Glorious and the Effulgent; nor could any mortal behold Him. A fire was flaming around Him. A fire also of great extent continued to rise up before Him; so that not one of those who surrounded Him was capable of approaching Him, among the myriads of 'myriads who were before Him. To Him holy consultation was needless. Yet did not the sanctified, who were near Him, depart far from Him either by night or by day; nor were they removed from Him. I also was so far advanced, with a veil on my face, and trembling. Then the Lord with his own mouth called me, saying, Approach hither, Enoch, at my holy word. And He raised me up, making me draw near even to the entrance. My eye was directed to the ground.

Enoch Chapter 15

Then addressing me, He spoke and said, Hear, neither be afraid, O righteous Enoch, thou scribe of righteousness: approach hither, and hear my voice. Go, say to the Watchers of heaven, who have sent thee to pray for them, You ought to pray for men, and not men for you. Wherefore have you forsaken the lofty and holy heaven, which endures forever, and have lain with women; have defiled yourselves with the daughters of men; have taken to yourselves wives; have acted like the sons of the earth, and have begotten an impious offspring? You being spiritual, holy, and possessing a life which is eternal, have polluted yourselves with women; have begotten in carnal blood; have lusted in the blood of men; and have done as those who are flesh and blood do. These however die and perish. Therefore have I given to them wives, that they might cohabit with them; that sons might be born of them; and that this might be transacted upon earth. But you from the beginning were made spiritual, possessing a life which is eternal, and not subject to death for ever. Therefore I made not wives for you, because, being spiritual, your dwelling is in heaven. Now the giants, who have been born of spirit and of flesh, shall be called upon earth evil spirits, and on earth shall be their habitation. Evil spirits shall proceed from their flesh, because they were created from above; from the holy Watchers was their beginning and primary foundation. Evil spirits shall they be upon earth, and the spirits of the wicked shall they be called. The habitation of the spirits of heaven shall be in heaven; but upon earth shall be the habitation of terrestrial spirits, who are born on earth. The spirits of the giants shall be like clouds, which shall oppress, corrupt, fall, contend, and bruise upon earth.

Evil Spirits

Now, let's look at this last verse. Verse eight tells us the spirits of these fallen giants, because they are a combination of flesh and spirit, will become what we now call "evil spirits." This section tells us these evil spirits will be like clouds, which is reminiscent of 2 Peter's discourse of the ungodly, where he writes in

2 Peter 2:17

> *"These are springs without water, and mists driven by a storm; for whom the blackness of darkness hath been reserved."*

These evil spirits have nobody to dwell in, they roam the earth looking for those they can inhabit. We see also from the above quote of the Book of Enoch, that these two-hundred original Watcher Angels, have been chained until the Day of Judgment.

However, these evil spirits, whose whole nature is to tempt and torment, are here on planet earth. These are those we wrestle with, for we "wrestle not against flesh and blood, but against Powers and Principalities and spiritual wickedness in heavenly places," according to Ephesians six. These evil spirits are still in process of carrying out the original intent of their leader, to rebel against and question God's Authority and purposes for creation.

We know from scripture all flesh was destroyed during the flood of Noah, except Noah and his family. And yet we see in Genesis six:

The Nephilim were on the earth in those days, and also afterward, when the sons of God came in to the daughters of men, and they bore children to them. Those were the mighty men who were of old, men of renown.

Noah lived three hundred and fifty years after the flood, according to Genesis 9:28.

Hundreds of years after the flood of Noah, we read in Numbers 13:30 when Moses sent the spies into the Promised land they encountered giants.

And Caleb stilled the people before Moses, and said, Let us go up at once, and possess it; for we are well able to overcome it. But the men that went up with him said, We be not able to go up against the people; for they are stronger than we. And they brought up an evil report of the land which they had searched unto the children of Israel, saying, The land, through which we have gone to search it, is a land that eateth up the inhabitants thereof; and all the people that we saw in it are men of a great stature. And there we saw the giants, the sons of Anak, which come of the giants: and we were in our own sight as grasshoppers, and so we were in their sight.

Moses slew King Og, whose coffin was thirteen and a half feet long and six feet wide.[5]

> *Deuteronomy 3:3-11 The Lord our God helped us destroy Og and his army and conquer his entire kingdom of Bashan, including the Argob region. His kingdom had lots of villages and sixty towns with high walls and gates that locked with bars. We completely destroyed them all, killing everyone, but keeping the livestock and everything else of value. Sihon and Og had ruled Amorite kingdoms east of the Jordan River. Their land stretched from the Arnon River gorge in the south to Mount Hermon in the north, and we captured it all. Mount Hermon is called Mount Sirion by the people of Sidon, and it is called Mount Senir by the Amorites. We captured all the towns in the highlands, all of Gilead, and all of Bashan as far as Salecah and Edrei, two of the towns that Og had ruled. King Og was the last of the Rephaim, (**one species of giant**) and his coffin is in the town of Rabbah in Ammon. It is made of hard black rock and is thirteen and a half feet long and six feet wide.(emphasis/insert mine) (thirteen feet by six feet according to: **www.convert-me.com**)*

According to this scripture, King Og was the last of the Rephaim, who were one of several tribes of giants occupying the land. God told Moses and Joshua to destroy them *all* because they were not "human" as God created humankind. These were a mutant combination of human DNA and fallen angel DNA.

David, who lived hundreds of years after Noah, slew Goliath, a giant, who according to I Samuel 17:4, was "six cubits and a span" tall.

A cubit by our measuring table is approximately eighteen inches and a span equals six inches, therefore "six cubits and a span" would put Goliath at approximately nine feet and six inches. The weight of his "coat of mail" was five thousand shekels of brass, by our measuring standards that would be approximately one-hundred and twenty-six pounds.[1]

Let's look at the particulars of this record.
> *Now the Philistines gathered together their armies to*
> *battle, and were gathered together at Shochoh, which*
> *[belongeth] to Judah, and pitched between Shochoh and*
> *Azekah, in Ephesdammim. And Saul and the men of*
> *Israel were gathered together, and pitched by the valley of*
> *Elah, and set the battle in array against the Philistines. And*
> *the Philistines stood on a mountain on the one side, and*
> *Israel stood on a mountain on the other side: and [there was]*
> *a valley between them. And there went out a champion out of*
> *the camp of the Philistines, named Goliath, of Gath, whose*
> *height [was] six cubits and a span. 5And [he had] an helmet of*
> *brass upon his head, and he [was] armed with a coat of*
> *mail; and the weight of the coat [was] five thousand shekels of*
> *brass. 6And [he had] greaves of brass upon his legs, and a*
> *target of brass between his shoulders. 7And the staff of his*
> *spear [was] like a weaver's beam; and his*
> *spear's head [weighed] six hundred shekels of iron:*

The battle with these inhabitants of Israel went on for years, many years later, when David was reigning as King of Israel, we see Israel still battling giants in the land.

1 Chronicles 20:4-8 (ASV)

And it came to pass after this, that there arose war at Gezer with the Philistines: then Sibbecai the Hushathite slew Sippai, of the sons of the giant; and they were subdued. And there was again war with the Philistines; and Elhanan the son of Jair slew Lahmi the brother of Goliath the Gittite, the staff of whose spear was like a weaver's beam. And there was again war at Gath, where was a man of great stature, whose fingers and toes were four and twenty, six on each hand, and six on each foot; and he also was born unto the giant. But when he defied Israel, Jonathan the son of Shimea David's brother slew him. These were born unto the giant in Gath; and they fell by the hand of David, and by the hand of his servants.

The book of Joshua records fierce battles with these beings.

Though Lucifer himself is bound in Tartarus, his offspring continue his assignment against Creation, mankind and our Creator God, through their earthly agents. The Luciferian Elite, Mystery Religions and Occultists get their orders from these beings who are carrying out the orders of Lucifer himself.

Our next step in tracing Lucifer's strategies against mankind, is to look at where they came from *after* the flood of Noah's time, which was intended to wipe them off the face of the earth.

The Luciferian Strategy

Chapter 4

ALL THINGS ARE NEW

After the flood of Noah's time there was a NEW Creation...behold all things were made new!

The Creator pushed the "reset" button and all things were restored to the original plan.

The only animals on planet earth now are the animals God created. There are no remnants of those produced by the fallen angels, the chimera, a mix of human seed with animal seed to create part animal, part human hybrids.

There are no giants left on the earth, now, once again the only mankind on planet earth are those God created.

The *only* thing remaining from the former creation are the spirits of the children of the fallen angels, and the remnants of the cities they built.

Sin is cleansed from the earth. All things have been made new!
And God spake unto Noah, saying;
Go forth of the ark, thou, and thy wife, and thy sons, and thy
sons' wives with thee. Bring forth with thee every living thing

that is with thee, of all flesh, both of fowl, and of cattle, and of every creeping thing that creepeth upon the earth; that they may breed abundantly in the earth, and be fruitful, and multiply upon the earth. And Noah went forth, and his sons, and his wife, and his sons' wives with him: Every beast, every creeping thing, and every fowl, and whatsoever creepeth upon the earth, after their kinds, went forth out of the ark.
Genesis 8:15-19

What an experience it must have been for Noah and his family as they stepped from the Ark that first day!

The earth itself would have been rejoicing! The very air they breathed, cleansed of corruption and made fresh, clean and new!

Imagine standing on the top of one of earths' highest mountain peaks, over-looking creation and breathing in the fresh new air!

Man is restored with a free-will, to choose to love and serve the God who created them with such Love.
The first thing Noah did was to build an Altar to the Lord   and present a sacrifice, wanting to please the Lord.

And Noah builded an altar unto Jehovah, and took of every clean beast, and of every clean bird, and offered burnt-offerings on the altar.
And Jehovah smelled the sweet savor; and Jehovah said in his heart, I will not again curse the ground any more for man's sake, for that the imagination of man's heart is evil from his

youth; neither will I again smite any more everything living, as I have done. Genesis 8:20-21 (ASV)

And the Lord received the sweet aroma of his sacrifice and responded by reestablishing His Covenant with mankind:

And God blessed Noah and his sons, and said unto them, Be fruitful, and multiply, and replenish the earth. And the fear of you and the dread of you shall be upon every beast of the earth, and upon every fowl of the air, upon all that moveth upon the earth, and upon all the fishes of the sea; into your hand are they delivered. Every moving thing that liveth shall be meat for you; even as the green herb have I given you all things. But flesh with the life thereof, which is the blood thereof, shall ye not eat. And surely your blood of your lives will I require; at the hand of every beast will I require it, and at the hand of man; at the hand of every man's brother will I require the life of man. Whoso sheddeth man's blood, by man shall his blood be shed: for in the image of God made he man. And you, be ye fruitful, and multiply; bring forth abundantly in the earth, and multiply therein. And God spake unto Noah, and to his sons with him, saying, And I, behold, I establish my covenant with you, and with your seed after you; And with every living creature that is with you, of the fowl, of the cattle, and of every beast of the earth with you; from all that go out of the ark, to every beast of the earth. And I will establish my covenant with you, neither shall all flesh be cut off any more by the waters of a flood; neither shall there anymore be a flood to destroy the earth. And God said, This is the token of the covenant which I make between me and you and every living creature that is with you, for perpetual generations: I do set my bow in the cloud, and it shall be for a token of a covenant between me and the earth. And it shall come to pass, when I bring a cloud over the earth, that the bow shall be seen in the cloud: And I will remember my covenant, which is between me and you and every living creature of all flesh; and the waters shall no more become a flood to destroy all flesh. And the bow shall be in the cloud; and I will look upon it, that I may remember the everlasting covenant between God and every living creature of all flesh that is upon the earth. And God said unto Noah, This is the token of the covenant, which I have established between me and all flesh that is upon the earth. **Genesis 9:1-17 (NIV).**

Can you imagine seeing the *first* Rainbow? The brilliance of the colors against the clean, clear blue of the sky must have been an amazing sight!

Ahh...all things *fresh* and *new*! I'm sure the Father Himself took a deep sigh of relief, along with all of His Angels who had watched the destruction of His original creation by their fallen counterparts during the previous millennia!

The Luciferian Strategy

Chapter 5

SIN REINTRODUCED

Everything on planet earth took a huge sigh of relief – except, I'm sure, for the spirits of the fallen giants, who were now roaming the earth looking for a host.

"Sin" is defined by the Google dictionary as:

> an immoral act considered to be a transgression against divine law. "a sin in the eyes of God" immoral
> act, wrong, wrongdoing, act of
> evil/wickedness, transgression, crime, offense, misdeed, mis
> demeanor,wickedness, wrongdoing, wrong, evil, evildoing, s
> infulness, immorality, iniquity, vice.

The "evil spirits" roaming the earth did not take long to find a willing host.
Genesis 9 goes on to record, after such an innocent, glorious beginning, mankind quickly fell, in the time it takes for a vineyard to produce grapes and ferment into wine.

> And the sons of Noah, that went forth from the ark, were Shem, and Ham, and Japheth: and Ham is the father of Canaan.

These three were the sons of Noah: and of these was the whole earth overspread. And Noah began to be a husbandman, and planted a vineyard: and he drank of the wine, and was drunken. And he was uncovered within his tent. And Ham, the father of Canaan, saw the nakedness of his father, and told his two brethren without. And Shem and Japheth took a garment, and laid it upon both their shoulders, and went backward, and covered the nakedness of their father. And their faces were backward, and they saw not their father's nakedness. And Noah awoke from his wine, and knew what his youngest son had done unto him. And he said, Cursed be Canaan; A servant of servants shall he be unto his brethren. And he said, Blessed be Jehovah, the God of Shem; And let Canaan be his servant. God enlarge Japheth, And let him dwell in the tents of Shem; And let Canaan be his servant. And Noah lived after the flood three hundred and fifty years. And all the days of Noah were nine hundred and fifty years: And he died. **Genesis 9:18-29 (ASV)**

According to [1]*Homeguides for wine growing*, it takes approximately three years to grow grapes ready for wine-making, and another thirty to forty days to actually make the wine. Therefore, within a very few years after cleansing the earth of debauchery and sin, mankind has once again given into the lusts of the flesh with the resulting consequences.

Remembering the definition of sin as "a transgression against divine law," even though it had not been put in writing, it had been communicated by God when He created man in His image – His reflection. Just as the birds of the air and beasts of the field knew instinctively, so man knew instinctively the heart of the Father.

> **Exodus 20:12 (ASV)**
> *Honor thy father and thy mother, that thy days may be long in the land which Jehovah thy God giveth thee.*

There is on-going historical debate whether Ham simply exposed the nakedness of his father or if he actually committed sodomy. Either way, in seeing the drunken, naked condition of his father, he was tempted to at least mock and make fun of him with his brothers. He succumbed to the temptation to bring dishonor to his father.

In so dishonoring his father, Ham had committed a grave sin, and he knew it.

Many commentators point out that Noah cursed Canaan the son of Ham, because Ham had been blessed by God, therefore Noah would not curse what God had blessed.

There is also debate whether by "debauchery" Noah, by getting falling down, naked drunk, opened the door and was the first to reintroduce agreement with the spirits of the enemy into the new earth.

While the New Testament had not yet been written, the *principles* of God's commands were written on the hearts of the Old Testament inhabitants.

Ephesians 5:18 (KJV)

And be not drunk with wine, wherein is excess; but be filled with the Spirit;

If we look at the word "excess", we find:
...a presumed derivative of <G4982> (sozo); properly *unsavedness*, i.e. (by implication) *profligacy* (excess, riot) Strong's Talking Greek & Hebrew Dictionary.
(incorrigibleness), an abandoned, dissolute, life; profligacy, prodigality

It would seem Noah had succumbed to his flesh.

The roaming evil spirits had found a host in Ham and now his son Canaan had been cursed, and became "easy pickings."

The Luciferian Strategy to destroy, or at the very least, corrupt God's creation, continued.

The Luciferian Strategy

Sin Reintroduced

Chapter 6

THE STEPS OF CANAAN

In following the steps of Canaan we see he occupied the land surrounding Mt. Hermon. This is the mountain recorded in Chapter seven of the Book of Enoch, where the fallen angels first landed on planet earth after agreeing together to leave their positions as Holy Watcher Angels:

Then they swore all together, and all bound themselves by mutual execrations. Their whole number was two hundred, who descended upon Ardis. That mountain therefore was called Armon, because they had sworn upon it, and bound themselves by mutual execrations.

Mt. Armon, or Mt. Hermon, derives its name from the Hebrew word herem, a curse.

> *Dictionaries - Hitchcock's Bible Names Dictionary - Hermon anathema; devoted to destruction*

According to New World Encyclopedia website[2] :

*Mount Hermon is a mountain in the Anti-Lebanon mountain range. Its highest point is 2,814 m (9,230 feet) above sea level. In the **Hebrew Bible**, Mount Hermon constituted part of the northern border of the Promised Land, and in the **Book of Enoch** it is the site of the descent of the* *fallen **angels** when they determined to take human wives on earth. In the **New Testament**, it is a likely candidate for the so-called "Mount of Transfiguration."*

According to :
http://www.biblestudytools.com/dictionary/hermon/
It (Mt. Hermon) is about 40 miles north of the Sea of Galilee.

According to:
http://www.newworldencyclopedia.org/entry/Mount_Hermon
In the New Testament, the Gospels tell of Jesus and his disciples journeying north from Bethsaida on the Sea of Galilee to the city of Caesarea Philippi, which lay at the southern base of Mount Hermon (Matthew 16:13). There, Jesus revealed to them his purpose to build his church and to go to Jerusalem to die and be resurrected (Matthew 16:18-21).

Jesus took His disciples to the top of Mt. Hermon to be transfigured before them, revealing Himself as the Son of the Living God, *connecting* Himself to God and the God-Head, in direct contrast to the enemy's having broken relationship with that same God-Head so many generations before. He also declared from that very location of rebellion:

Matthew 16:17-19 (KJV)

And Jesus answered and said unto him, Blessed art thou, Simon Barjona: for flesh and blood hath not revealed it unto thee, but my Father which is in heaven. And I say also unto thee, That thou art Peter, and upon this rock I will build my church; and

the gates of hell shall not prevail against it. And I will give unto
thee the keys of the kingdom of heaven: and whatsoever thou
shalt bind on earth shall be bound in heaven: and whatsoever
thou shalt loose on earth shall be loosed in heaven.

Now, this is *strictly* conjecture on my part...but, could it be, Jesus
intentionally took His Disciples to that very Gate so that He could
Decree from that very Gate of rebellion the *reclaiming* of Creation
once and for all "upon this rock - this very Gate of rebellion - I
build my church and the Gates of hell *will not prevail* against it."
In the book of Romans we are told:

For the creation waits in eager expectation for the children of
God to be revealed. For the creation was subjected to
frustration, not by its own choice, but by the will of the one
who subjected it, in hope that the creation itself will be
liberated from its bondage to decay and brought into the
freedom and glory of the children of God. We know that the
whole creation has been groaning as in the pains of childbirth
right up to the present time.

I imagine the part of creation now named Mt. Hermon, breathed
a huge sigh of relief that day, as Jesus Himself, the very Word that
created it in the first place, reconnected it with its' Creator. The
very spot on planet earth that was the beginning of iniquity and
corruption, had that day, become *the* location of heavenly Glory.
Jesus brought redemption to Mt. Hermon from the curse of the
iniquity brought to it, through the rebellion of the formally
heavenly beings, so many generations before.

Back to Ham and his generations

But, in the time of Ham and his son Canaan it was a place of possible power.

Ham had fallen into disrepute with his father and brothers and his son was now cursed by God. Sin, bound in the heart of men from their youth according to Genesis:

> *...for that the imagination of man's heart is evil from his youth Genesis 8:20-21*

Ham and his sons began looking for ways to "succeed".

God was against them. Their family disapproved of them.
They were now ripe pickings for the roaming enemy to inspire them to join in their rebellion.

The Luciferian Strategy

The Steps Of Canaan

Chapter 7

HAM AND HIS DESCENDANTS

We're going to pick up the story of Ham and his descendants from the book of Jubilees.

Understanding the book of Jubilees is not in the accepted Canon of Scripture, we will use Scripture to confirm truth.

Psalm 119:160 states the entirety of God's Word is truth. Starting with that premise, we can compare writings outside of the accepted Canon of Scripture to see if they meet the criteria.

As an example, the Bible states that Jesus Christ is God
Isaiah 9:6-7; Matthew 1:22-23; John 1:1, 2, 14, 20:28; Acts 16:31, 34; Philippians 2:5-6; Colossians 2:9; Titus 2:13; Hebrews 1:8; 2 Peter 1:1.

Many extra-biblical texts, claiming to be Scripture, argue that Jesus is *not* God. The Book of Jubilees is not one of them.

When clear contradictions exist, the established Bible is to be trusted.

There are many details of history not included in Canonized Scripture, which are included in "extra-biblical" works, as long as these agree with the accepted Word of God they help us get a fuller picture of the story of History.

The History of Canaan

Now let's track the lineage of Canaan.

In Jubilees we find:

And he (Canaan) found a writing which former (generations) had carved on the rock, and he read what was thereon, and he transcribed it and sinned owing to it; for it contained the teaching of the Watchers in accordance with which they used to observe the omens of the sun and moon and stars in all the signs of heaven. And he wrote it down and said nothing regarding it; for he was afraid to speak to Noah about it lest he should be angry with him on account of it.

Ham was the father of Canaan.

> **Genesis 9:18**
> *Now the sons of Noah who came out of the ark were Shem and Ham and Japheth;* **and Ham was the father of Canaan.** *(emphasis mine)*

Canaan was the father of Nimrod: Gen. 10:7 – 9 confirms this;
> *Genesis 10:7 The sons of Cush were Seba and Havilah and Sabtah and Raamah and Sabteca; and the sons of Raamah were Sheba*

and Dedan. 8 Now Cush became the father of Nimrod; he became a mighty one on the earth. 9He was a mighty hunter before the LORD; therefore it is said, "Like Nimrod a mighty hunter before the LORD."...New American Standard Bible

Cush, also spelled as Kush, (/kʊʃ, kʌʃ/; Biblical: כּוּשׁ Kûš) was, according to the Bible, the eldest son of Ham, who was a son of Noah. He was the brother of Canaan (land of Canaan), Mizraim (Egypt) and Phut (land of Libya), and the father of the Biblical Nimrod mentioned in the "Table of Nations" in the Genesis 10:6 and I Chronicles 1:8. Cush is traditionally considered the eponymous ancestor of the people of the "land of Cush," an ancient territory that is believed to have been located on either side or both sides of the Red Sea. As such, "Cush" is alternately identified in Scripture with the Kingdom of Kush, ancient Sudan, and/or the Arabian Peninsula.[1]
https://en.wikipedia.org/wiki/Cush_(Bible)

Matthew Henry Commentary on Nimrod: 10:8-14
*Nimrod was a great man in his day; he began to be mighty in the earth. Those before him were content to be upon the same level with their neighbors, and though every man bare rule in his own house, yet no man pretended any further. Nimrod was resolved to lord it over his neighbors. **The spirit of the giants before the flood, who became mighty men, and men of renown, Genesis 6:4, revived in him.** Nimrod was a great hunter. Hunting then was the method of preventing the hurtful increase of wild beasts.*

*This required great courage and address, and thus gave an opportunity for Nimrod to command others, and gradually attached a number of men to one leader. (**emphasis mine**)*

From such a beginning, it is likely, that Nimrod began to rule, and to force others to submit. He invaded his neighbours' rights and properties, and persecuted innocent men; endeavouring to make all his own by force and violence. He carried on his oppressions and violence in defiance of God himself. Nimrod was a great ruler. Some way or other, by arts or arms, he got into power, and so founded a monarchy, which was the terror of the mighty, and bid fair to rule all the world. Nimrod was a great builder. Observe in Nimrod the nature of ambition. It is boundless; much would have more, and still cries, Give, give. It is restless; Nimrod, when he had four cities under his command, could not be content till he had four more.

It is expensive; Nimrod would rather be in charge of rearing cities, than not have the honour of ruling them. It is daring, and will stop at nothing. Nimrod's name signifies rebellion; tyrants to men are rebels to God. The days are coming, when conquerors will no longer be spoken of with praise, as in man's partial histories, but be branded with infamy, as in the impartial records of the Bible.

Genesis 10:8 says about Nimrod:

> *And Cush begat Nimrod: he began to be a mighty one in the earth.*

Dr. Tom Horn comments on this verse:

"Three sections in this unprecedented verse indicate something very peculiar happened to Nimrod. First, note where the text says, "he began to be." In Hebrew, this is chalal, which means "to become profaned, defiled, polluted, or desecrated ritually, sexually or genetically." Second, this verse tells us exactly what Nimrod began to be as he changed genetically—"a mighty one" (gibbowr, gibborim), one of the offspring of Nephilim.

As Annette Yoshiko Reed says in the Cambridge University book, *Fallen Angels and the History of Judaism and Christianity*, "The Nephilim of Genesis 6:4 are always...grouped together with the gibborim as the progeny of the Watchers and human women." And the third part of this text says the change to Nimrod started while he was on "earth."

Therefore, in modern language, this text could accurately be translated to say: "And Nimrod began to change genetically, becoming a gibborim, the offspring of watchers on earth."
http://www.newswithviews.com/Horn/thomas155.htm

The Luciferian Strategy freely flowing through Nimrod

Nimrod is now armed with the forbidden technology of the Watcher Angels, making a name for himself and ruling as King. Lucifer's strategies through the ages all flow back to Nimrod. To this very day, Archeologists funded by the Esoteric Elite are searching for any connection they can find to Nimrod and the Tower of Babel.

Lucifer, now chained in Tartarus, but aware of events on the surface of planet earth through the spirits of his offspring, must have been elated with Nimrod. Once again he had access to God's highest Creation. Once again he had opportunity to destroy and corrupt. Just as at the Crucifixion, he thought he had won against the very God who created Him with such love and perfection. In his jealousy and pride, he had become the Adversary to the very Creator God, who created with such love.

Tower of Babel

Genesis 11:1-9

> *And the whole earth was of one language, and of one speech. And it came to pass, as they journeyed from the east, that they found a plain in the land of Shinar; and they dwelt there. And they said one to another, Go to, let us make brick, and burn them thoroughly. And they had brick for stone, and slime had they for mortar. And they said, Go to, let us build us a city and a tower, whose top may reach unto heaven; and let us make us a name, lest we be scattered abroad upon the face of the whole earth. And the Lord came down to see the city and the tower, which the children of men builded. And the Lord said, Behold, the people is one, and they have all one language; and this they begin to do:* **and now nothing will be restrained from them, which they have imagined to do**. *Go to, let us go down, and there confound their language, that they may not understand one another's speech. So*

the Lord scattered them abroad from thence upon the face of all the earth: and they left off to build the city. Therefore is the name of it called Babel; because the Lord did there confound the language of all the earth: and from thence did the Lord scatter them abroad upon the face of all the earth.

King James Version (KJV) Public Domain (emphasis mine)

Here we have the Father interrupting the Luciferian Strategy to destroy mankind, just as He Mercifully has done through the ages. In the New Testament we are told in Matthew 24:21-22 (KJV):

For then shall be great tribulation, such as was not since the beginning of the world to this time, no, nor ever shall be. And except those days should be shortened, there should no flesh be saved: ***but for the elect's sake those days shall be shortened. (emphasis mine)***

For the elect's sake the coming days of Tribulation will be shortened and for the elect's sake the plan of Nimrod was thwarted. We serve a loving Father!

Through various writings, researchers have realized that in fact, the Tower of Babel was not built with the intent of the building itself "reaching into heaven", *but* that it would enable them to connect to and contact the Second heaven dwelling place of the Demonic.

Mankind's Migration

Now mankind was spread across the earth, carrying with them various diluted forms of Idol worship taught by Nimrod. These evil incantations and wicked enchantments became the groundwork for evil across the earth.

The Tree of the Knowledge of Good and Evil

When Eve rebelled against the Command of God and ate of the fruit of the Tree of the Knowledge of Good and Evil, she gave access to Lucifer to reveal to mankind all of its' secrets. Just as a loving Father would never put a loaded gun in the hand of his three year old child or put him behind the wheel of a car driving down a highway, so our Father preserves some things in secret until we are ready to handle them. Lucifer however, delights in putting mankind in a position of Authority and Power before he is able to process the results effectively.

The Tree of the Knowledge of Good and Evil had locked within its fruit the Laws of Creation, the governing Principles of Good and Evil. This is WHY our loving Father told man *not* to eat of its' fruit, He knew we could not handle such knowledge. He knew what man has only recently discovered, "Power corrupts and absolute Power corrupts absolutely." Our Father, from a heart of Love evicted mankind from the Garden and posted a Fiery Angel to keep him from returning and eating of the Tree of Life and thereby living eternally with such corrupt Power.

Some ask, "Well, if God is so all powerful why doesn't he just STOP the enemy!" "Why did God create Lucifer and the Angels with the ability to choose?" "Why did God create man with the ability to choose right from wrong if He knows how much destruction it can bring?" Those that ask such questions don't understand the *whole* counsel and nature of our Father. They don't understand His Justice, His Righteousness. He *said* man was created in His image, His likeness. He is a being who can and does make *choices.* He has the power of Will, and He gave that power to mankind, He will not take it away. He allows us to make our choices and have the consequences of those choices, both for good and bad. When we, as an act of our Free Will, give our lives back to Him, and invite Him into our hearts and life and receive the empowering of His Holy Spirit, we receive and acknowledge *His* Lordship and not our own. In making that decision we are breaking agreement with the Luciferian Strategy to separate us from our Father. When we make

poor choices, and ask God for forgiveness and the ability to make *good* choices, we begin our journey back to our loving Father. When we come to Him in repentance and ask forgiveness He, in His faithfulness to His Promise, throws that sin as far as east is from the west, (which science has shown cannot be measured) *never* to recall it again.

It's been asked, "Why did God allow Satan to tempt Eve?" To such questions I have to ask, "What is the preciousness, the joy of love, if it is not freely given?" If Eve were programmed to obey, rather than *choose* to obey, if love is not a *choice* what is its impact?

When my children were young and they obeyed, not out of fear, but from a heart of love, because they respected and loved my husband and I, it blessed us. When I'm told that I'm loved by a dear friend or family member or my precious husband, it *warms* my heart, it *blesses* me, as it does you when your loved ones express their love and appreciation of you.

Freely given love and appreciation from us blesses our Father God in the same way.

As humans, created in His image, when we *choose* to love and from that place of love, to obey, it opens the way for the Father to release the blessings, the consequences, of obedience. He has *chosen* to love us, and from that place of love, He even limits Himself to obey our choice of Will and to release its consequences to us, both for good and for evil. Love is a precious gift of ourselves to one another and to Him.

The Luciferian Strategy

Han And His Descendants

Chapter 8

THE TREE OF THE KNOWLEDGE OF GOOD AND EVIL

Locked in the fruit of the Tree of The Knowledge of Good and Evil was the knowledge of the DNA, which mankind is only now discovering. Locked in its fruit was the knowledge of the Soul and its power. Locked in its fruit was the knowledge of the heavens and their prophetic role and voice. Locked in its' fruit was the power of sound and color, the meaning of the Constellations and their Courses. Its' fruit contained the secrets of plant life and metallurgy and energy.

And now, even after the flood sent to erase the corruption of the rebellious, now, all of this knowledge was once again accessible to mankind through the incantations and enchantments found on the tablets discovered at the top of Mt. Hermon by Canaan. These communication methods for contacting the spirits of the descendants of the Fallen Angels, who had access to these secrets of Creation, were now accessed by Canaan, who had become convinced by the demonic entities now freely flowing in his bloodline, that he had been unjustly cursed and ostracized.
Josephus recorded: *"...discovered the science of the heavenly bodies and their orderly array. Moreover, to prevent their discoveries from being lost to mankind and perishing before they become known – Adam having predicted a destruction of the universe, at one time by*

a violent fire and at another by a mighty deluge of water – they erected two pillars, one of brick and the other of stone, and inscribed these discoveries on both; so that, if the pillar of brick disappeared in the deluge, that of stone would remain to teach men what was graven thereon and to inform them that they had also erected one of brick."[3]

DNA manipulation again produced Giants in the land[4], as recorded repeatedly in scripture:

Numbers 13:32-33 (KJV)
And they brought up an evil report of the land which they had searched unto the children of Israel, saying, The land, through which we have gone to search it, is a land that eateth up the inhabitants thereof; and all the people that we saw in it are men of a great stature. And there we saw the giants, the sons of Anak, which come of the giants: and **we were in our own sight as grasshoppers, and so we were in their sight.** (emphasis mine)

Genesis **6:4-5** *tells of the Nephilim before and after the Flood. According to Genesis 7:23, the Nephilim were destroyed in the Flood, but Nephilim are reported after the Flood, including:*
- *the Anakites (Numbers 13:28-33)*
- *the Emites (Deuteronomy 2:10)*
- *the Amorites (Amos 2:9)*[2]
- *the Rephaites (Joshua 12:4)*

The Nephilim, we now know, returned due to Ham's passing on and teaching his discoveries on the top of Mt. Hermon.

The Book of Numbers includes the discouraging report by the spies which Moses sent into Canaan. **The** Anakites are described as making the Israelites seem like grasshoppers (Numbers 13:33).

> *"We can't attack those people; they are stronger than we are.*
> *(...)*
> *All the people we saw there are of great size. We saw the Nephilim there (the descendants of Anak come from the Nephilim). We seemed like grasshoppers in our own eyes, and we looked the same to them."*

However, the Book of Joshua, describing the actual conquest of Canaan in a later generation, makes no reference to such people living there.

The Bible also tells of Gog and Magog, who are believed by some scholars to have later entered into European folklore, and of the famous battle between David and the Philistine Goliath.

Jewish historian Flavius Josephus also described the Amorites as giants in his Antiquities of the Jews, circa 93 AD, indicating that fossil evidence still remained at that time:[5]

> "For which reason they removed their camp to Hebron; and when they had taken it, they slew all the inhabitants. There were till then left the race of giants, who had bodies so large, and countenances so entirely

different from other men, that they were surprising to the sight, and terrible to the hearing. The bones of these men are still shown to this very day, unlike to any credible relations of other men."[5]

The Spread of Evil:
We see clearly the record of giant mutations in the land of Israel in the record of Scripture. But, in order to find if in fact, this knowledge of the corruption of creation was widespread, we have to look to extra-biblical texts. In every culture throughout the earth, there are stories of "Titans", giants, "mythological beings" of half-man half- animal.

Egyptian hieroglyphics, Greek "Myths", Japanese giants and Pyramids, Aztec Indian drawings, Myan Indian glyphs, American Indian lore. All tell of the same beings.

When we are told the Fallen Angels exchanged knowledge for women, we can make the mistake of rushing past that information and not look at, and realize the enormity of that information.

Angels can*not* create, but they know and understand the foundations of creation and the elements of the universe and earth. They *know* the Creators purposes and reasons for each element of creation.

One small example, "the heavens were created to declare the Glory of the Lord." Which tells us, if we read carefully, that the heavens have a voice. Science has only, in very recent times, discovered that stars do in fact release a sound. The enemy can capture that sound, using the empowerment of the Government of God given to mankind to rule over *all* of creation. He knows God will not go back on His Word. The enemy looks for willing, rebellious, power-hungry mankind, whom he can teach to capture that sound and pervert it from its' original purpose, and cause it to speak *his* words.

Locked in the Tree of Knowledge of Good and Evil were the secrets of Herbs and trees, fruit bearing trees and grass:

> *Gen 1:11 And God said, Let the earth bring forth grass, the herb yielding seed, and the fruit tree yielding fruit **after his kind**, <u>whose seed is in itself</u>, upon the earth: and it was so. **(emphasis mine)***

Today we have huge Agriculture companies mixing the seed of a tomato with that of fish to make a "bigger, better" tomato. The Luciferian message behind these "improvements" is that God didn't do it "good enough" we, mankind, can improve upon creation. We can create bigger, better ears of corn. We can improve our own DNA and thereby live longer, healthier lives.
What the manipulators of this kind of thinking don't want us to see or focus on is the epidemic-like outbreak of cancers and new diseases. Our God-created bodies simply do not know how to process these new genes thrust upon it. Those that speak up are labeled "conspiracy theorists". Academics who speak up lose their Tenure. Those in Industry who speak up are replaced.

Nothing our Father does is done by happenstance, as we know in our personal lives and walk with Him, every jot and tittle of our lives have purpose and meaning, so when He said in Genesis 1:12:

> *And the earth brought forth grass, and herb yielding seed after his kind, and the tree yielding fruit, whose seed was in itself, after his kind: and God saw that it was good.*

We can see as we look at Creation, the *goodness* of "each after its' own kind." The Father knew, what some are coming to know in this day, that there is a *purpose,* a *goodness* in each element of Creation functioning "after its' own kind." As we look at scripture, we get a glimpse of the purposes of the various forms of Creation.

One glimpse into the purposes of Creation in scripture is found in Psalm 148:

> *Praise ye the LORD. Praise ye the LORD from the heavens: praise him in the heights. Praise ye him, all his angels: praise ye him, all his hosts. Praise ye him, sun and moon: praise him, all ye stars of light. Praise him, ye heavens of heavens, and ye waters that be above the heavens. Let them praise the name of the LORD: for he commanded, and they were created. He hath also stablished them forever and ever: he hath made a decree which shall not pass. Praise the LORD from the earth, ye dragons, and all deeps: Fire, and hail; snow, and vapour; stormy wind fulfilling his word: Mountains, and all hills; fruitful trees, and all cedars: Beasts, and all cattle; creeping things, and flying fowl: Kings of the earth, and all people; princes, and all judges of the earth: Both*

young men, and maidens; old men, and children: Let them praise the name of the LORD: for his name alone is excellent; his glory is above the earth and heaven. He also exalteth the horn of his people, the praise of all his saints; even of the children of Israel, a people near unto him. Praise ye the LORD.

We can see from studying just this one scripture that the *purpose* of all of Creation, including mankind and "Kings of the earth", was to Praise the Lord.

We can see, if we are to believe His Word, and hopefully we do, that *everything* was given a voice. Voice, sound, was given with the *purpose* to Praise the Creator, *not* because He is an egomaniac, but because He knows if we give HIM the Praise due His Name we *won't* be in any agreement with our Adversary.

If we don't function in agreement with our Adversary, he will not be able to steal our purposes, kill our dreams and bodies, or destroy our relationships. The Father, in His Love for us, wants the best for us. Which does not mean that we will live out our time here on planet earth trouble free, if we totally submit to and love Him. This realm is not the Heavenly realm, as long as we are in this realm, we *are* in an eternal battle. Battlefields are messy and problematic. But as we walk through this time here in this realm, in submission to His Will and His Way, He is *always* with us to help and strengthen and encourage us.

Angels know this. Holy Angels rejoice at this knowledge and join with all of Creation to Praise His Name.

Now imagine a corrupt, rebellious, fallen angel with this knowledge. Imagine how it grieves them to hear Creation praising the very one they hate so intensely and gave up *everything* to try to rebel against.

The Fallen Angels, who "left their first estate" are locked in Tartarus, but the spirits of their corrupt offspring, because they have eternal life in their DNA were left roaming the earth after the flood. These "evil spirits" found a host in Ham and his offspring. Now, through their offspring and those they influence, they are free to once again reveal the secrets of Creation with the purpose of corrupting its' original intent.

We see evidence of this corruption throughout the earth, in every culture Archeologists have discovered similar glyphs. Every culture has stories of the perversion of creation and its' creatures. Chimera, the mixing of human and animal, are found in the history of cultures around the earth. Greek and Egyptian "Mythology" tell of Titans and giants, along with Aztec and Myan history as well as glyphs on the wall of the Grand Canyon.

Alchemy
The mystery of Alchemy, the mixing of herbs to cause an hallucinogenic state whereby the soul can enter another dimension and commune with evil spirits, and be "inspired" with "creativity" is a demonic inspiration. This "creativity" has brought the earth the corruption of the Occult. The releasing of these "inspired" ideas into the earth has caused the corruption of societies worldwide.

The Stars and Heavens
Genesis 1:14-18 (KJV)

> *And God said, Let there be lights in the firmament of the heaven to divide the day from the night; and let them be for signs, and for seasons, and for days, and years: And let them be for lights in the firmament of the heaven to give light upon the earth: and it was so. And God made two great lights; the greater light to rule the day, and the lesser light to rule the night: he made the stars also. And God set them in the firmament of the heaven to give light upon the earth, And to rule over the day and over the night,* and to divide the light from the darkness: and God saw that it was good.

The heavens, the Constellations were created to rule. The Fallen Angels knew this, and knew how to use that ability. This knowledge is embedded in their DNA, now passed on to evil spirits, who teach the corruption of this power to their adherents, in exchange for their souls and devotion.

Remember, evil spirits *need* the cooperation of mankind and their Authority. These evil spirits entice mankind to partner with them in the misuse of the original intent of the Constellations. Horoscopes came into cultures around the world through the inspiration of these evil spirits. The ensnaring of the power of the Solstice and Eclipses, the perverting of the meaning of the Signs in the Heavens are the work of the Occultic groups worldwide.

Mankind to rule the earth:
Psalm 115:15-16 (KJV)

Ye are blessed of the LORD which made heaven and earth.
[16] The heaven, even the heavens, are the LORD'S but the earth hath he given to the children of men

Genesis 1:26 (KJV)

And God said, Let us make man in our image, after our likeness: and let them have dominion over the fish of the sea, and over the fowl of the air, and over the cattle, and over all the earth, and over every creeping thing that creepeth upon the earth.

The earth also has a voice. The Occultist ensnare that voice through incantations performed by their adherents. Through these incantations they dedicate locations and raise Occultic Idol Altars to idols and gods who are no Gods. These dedications are accomplished through ceremonial activities, which may or may not include the shedding of the blood of animals or human sacrifice.

Everything "after its' kind."
God does not waste *one* word. Knowing this, we have to ask, why, after *every* category of Creation does scripture record it as created, "after its' kind?"
The Father was telling those with ears to hear, the *importance* of *not* mixing the seed of one creation with another. He *knew* the havoc it would bring.
But, the rebellious don't listen. The rebellious would rather "make their own way." The rebellious don't "seek wisdom in wise counsel", as scripture exhorts us to. The rebellious don't willingly surrender their Will. The rebellious have their Will slowly taken

from them in increments, like boiling frogs, with the false promise of whatever it is that is promised making them "feel better." The by-word of the Occult is "do whatever makes you feel good." No "constraints". The Occult convince potential victims that God wants to ruin their fun. God wants to spoil their life and keep them from having fun and doing "their own thing."

Chapter 9

LUCIFER THE THIEF

Jesus, knowing the true nature of Lucifer, rightly called him a "thief".

> *John 10:10:*
> *The thief cometh not, but for to steal, and to kill, and to destroy: I am come that they might have life, and that they might have it more abundantly.*

But, why? Why would Jesus call the Adversary a "thief?" What is the enemy trying to steal?

Knowing our original purpose and call to Rule the earth, these demonic, evil spirits, these offspring of the fallen angels are determined to keep us in subjugation. To *steal* that Authority from us by lying to the gullible, the rebellious, the power-hungry and telling them *they*, the evil spirits, have all power which they will share with them in exchange for servile worship.

For those with eyes to see, it's easy to see the enemy kill and destroy. When someone is murdered, we can see the hand of the enemy living out his goal in killing. When true destruction comes to a life or a community, we can easily see the hand of the enemy as the destroyer. But it takes clearer vision to see the Adversary functioning in his role of Thief in the stealing of *purpose.* We see a life lived through the demonic inspiration of "whatever feels good", we see a life ruled by "what's in it for me?", "what about ME?" and sometimes fail to see the waste of purpose and fulfillment of design.

With the hope of entrapping the innocent minded, the enemy lies with enticing promises of popularity, acceptance, ease, fame and every other goal of our fallen human nature. Our fallen nature, inherited from Adam, seeks its' original state *before* the fall. The original state of man was one of ease, we lived in a garden we tended, but which was immediately responsive. We lived in a condition of Glory, clothed in the very Glory of God. We lived in a condition where *all* of creation acknowledged us and submitted to our Authority. We lived in relationships where we were fully delighted in and accepted.

We so took God for granted that when the enemy came with his enticing lies, we succumbed...maybe there was *more*...maybe God *is* holding out on us!

And today those lies haven't changed and neither has our foolish nature. Before knowing anything about our Father God, before coming into a relationship with Him and getting to know Him we prejudge Him. The enemy whispers God is holding out on us, he whispers God wants to rule us and keep us under His thumb and ruin all our fun...and we decide to *try* "breaking the rules" ...just to *see.* We know "right" from "wrong" because God mercifully planted it in our hearts to *try* to keep us from having the end results of having our own will done. But, by the time we see the results of our decision to "try out" making our own choices, it's too late, we're hooked. We think the thought to just try smoking this one time so we'll look "cool" and fit in with our "friends", is *our* idea.

We don't realize we're being enticed from an outside source...next thing we know, we *have* to have a cigarette. We'll try "just ONE joint" ...next thing we know, we are selling a treasured keepsake to buy a stash.
And so it continues. Step by step the enemy whispers enticements we are convinced are our own independent ideas, leading us step by step away from our Father and His Divine purposes for our life. Purposes that lead to true fulfillment. Purposes and plans that lead to all of the success we could ever hope for! His Word is full of His promises toward those who are in relationship with Him.

The enemy uses everything at his disposal to attempt to keep us ignorant of the goodness of God. He uses all of the means of the world surrendered to him to entice us away from the knowledge of the true nature of God. He even uses Religion. His religious spirits abound in churches worldwide, telling followers all of the things they have to do in order to be made acceptable before God. Adherents are told to cut their hair or let their hair grow – depending on the culture, dress according to their interpretation of modest – and what is "appropriate" in one culture is totally IN-appropriate in another! Behavior must conform. Speech must conform. There is a "Christianese" language that is used throughout much of the Church that has nothing to do with our Fathers' heart. The intent and purpose of the enemy through "religion" is to steal the worship, the intimacy designed for God and His children. In Religion there are prayers prayed to various deities, to various "intermediaries" who have *nothing* to do with God. These prayers, this worship is being offered by sincere, innocent hearts, who *think* they're praying to God, not knowing their prayers, intercession and worship is being hijacked by a god who is no God. When their prayers go unanswered or life is one calamity after another they blame God, feeling as though they had done *everything* they knew to do, and God just didn't care. The enemy rejoices, while our Father is moving heaven and earth to get the Truth to them.

> **Hebrews 11:6 (KJV)**
> *But without faith it is impossible to please him: for he that cometh to God must believe that he is, and that he is a rewarder of them that diligently seek him.*

"Self-righteousness" is the command of Religion. We're ordered to clean ourselves up before we can come before a Holy God. We're told to stop sinning and begin living holy lives by an enemy who knows that without Faith it is impossible to please God. When Jesus was asked this question by those around Him, He answered:

> **John 6:28-30 (KJV)**
> *Then said they unto him, What shall we do, that we might work the works of God?*
> *29 Jesus answered and said unto them, This is the work of* **God,** *that ye believe on him whom he hath sent.*
> **(emphasis mine)**

This is "Faith" – *believing* Jesus is Who God says He is. The enemy has his adherents in Religion believing Jesus is everything from Michael the Arch Angel or one of many Prophets to just one of many "Saviors." The enemy and his Religions have depicted Jesus and God as too high, too Holy to be approachable so we, lowly mankind, laymen, need "intermediaries" to approach God on our behalf. While the Truth from God's Word is:

> *John 3:16-21 (KJV)*
> *For God the world so loved, that he **gave** his only begotten Son, that **whosoever** believeth in him should not perish, but have everlasting life. For God sent not his Son into the world to condemn the world; but that the world through him might be saved. He that believeth on him is not condemned: but he that believeth not is condemned already, because he hath not believed in the name of the only begotten Son of God. And **this** is the condemnation, that **light is come into the world, and men loved darkness rather than light,** because their deeds were evil. For every one that doeth evil hateth the light, neither cometh to the light, lest his deeds should be reproved. But he that doeth truth cometh to the light, that his deeds may be made manifest, that they are wrought in God.(**emphasis mine**)*

Our Father is approachable. He gave His finest, His only Son, to undo the sin of Adam and restore a relationship with mankind. Our enemy has steadfastly preyed upon the foolishness bound in the heart of men to lie to them of our Father's intentions toward us.

Rather than our going to our Father and finding out for ourselves what He has to say, we have believed the word of his sworn enemy to interpret His heart. The relationship the Father has so tried to establish with us has been stolen by the Thief through the generations, and continues to be corrupted, except by the comparable few, the "remnant" who pursue Him. The enemy does *not* want the followers of Jesus to *know* who they are.

Those he loses to the Truth, those who do manage to come into relationship with the Father through Jesus, the enemy judiciously pursues to keep from learning the Truth of who they are in Jesus! We are Priests, Kings – and NOT just in "the next life," but here, now. WE are His Ambassadors on Planet Earth. In the natural when a Nation sends an Ambassador to another Nation, wherever that Ambassador is, is the Nation he comes from. His dwelling is his native land in that foreign land. The laws of his homeland prevail wherever he is assigned. How much more those of us who are heavenly Ambassadors.

2 Corinthians 5:19-20 (KJV)

To wit, that God was in Christ, reconciling the world unto himself, not imputing their trespasses unto them; and hath committed unto us the word of reconciliation. Now then we are ambassadors for Christ, as though God did beseech you by us: we pray you in Christ's stead, be ye reconciled to God.

And even more, Jesus Himself has said:

Luke 10:18-19 (KJV)

And he said unto them, I beheld Satan as lightning fall from heaven. Behold, I give unto you power to tread on serpents

*and scorpions, and over all the power of the enemy: and
nothing shall by any means hurt you.*

The enemy *really* doesn't want us to learn the Authority we have
over *all* of his power. Yes, he has power, but the Lord has given
those who follow Him *all* Authority over that power. He can do
nothing without our allowing, our agreement.

When Jesus said:

Matthew 16:18 (KJV)
*...And I say also unto thee, That thou art Peter, and upon this rock
I will build my church; **and the gates of hell shall not prevail
against it.(emphasis mine)***

If a thorough search of the word here used as "church" is done, you
will discover it is the same meaning as the term used for the
Sanhedrin in Israel. When Jesus said, "...I will build my church" He
was saying on this belief Peter had just expressed, and from Mt.
Hermon, the very place of rebellion and corruption of purpose,
that Jesus was the Son of God, that He would build His Ruling
Council, His Sanhedrin, on that belief.

We are to rule and reign in earth affairs, but Lucifer has convinced
those he could keep away from the Truth of Who Jesus is, that our
only function is to believe on Jesus. If the enemy could not keep us
from learning the truth then he would do the next best thing and
convince us to simply live a "good, quiet life," die and go to heaven,
and by all means *"stay out of being entangled with the world!"* Our
enemy wants us as disconnected from the decision making
processes on this earth as possible. Yes, Jesus said:

John 17:14-16 (KJV) I have given them thy word; and the world hath hated them, because they are not of the world, even as I am not of the world. ***I pray not that thou shouldest take them out of the world, but that thou shouldest keep them from the evil.*** *They are not of the world, even as I am not of the world. **(emphasis mine)***

When we come to Jesus, acknowledging Him to be Who He is, we "are a new creation", we are no longer "of this world." Jesus prayed that *we would be kept from the evil of the world system,* the system that doesn't acknowledge Him as Who He is. The system the enemy inspires to remain self-gratifying, never surrendered to its' Creator. The System the enemy uses to entice his followers to come into lock-step with each other. To conform to the "politically correct" mindset. To conform to the "socially acceptable" behavior. The System totally opposed to surrender and submission to a loving Creator God who delights in our uniqueness and individuality. The key word is "conform" – the total anti-thesis to our Father, who created each of us with our own set of fingerprints, unique. The enemy hates our uniqueness because he can't control uniqueness, you never know what Uniqueness will do!

Our Father created each of us unique and *delights* in our uniqueness as it is relinquished to Him. As our uniqueness is relinquished to Him and His Lordship it is able to be expressed in fullness, to fulfill all He had in mind when He created us. The enemy knows this and does all he can to destroy that very seed of creativity and if not to destroy it to pervert it for his own uses. Therefore for instance, we have individuals created with a seed of music in their being, and the enemy distorts its purposes and the world winds up with "Gangsta Rap", rather than a unique sound carrying the Truth of Who Jesus is to new generations. Art, Fashion, Industry, Education, you name the Genre' and if you look with eyes to see the distortion, you see the enemy's destruction of purpose and promise at work. At the same time, if you look with eyes to see the seed of creativity planted by the Father, you see the beauty of Creation expressed in every arena. You see those gifted with prowess giving Glory to their creator on the Sports' fields. You see Fashion expressing the beauty of Femininity for woman and Masculinity for men. You hear music that transcends your soul to its Creator, photos and movies displaying the wonders of creation. You see our Father delighting in His children.

Jesus knew the depth of the truth He spoke when He called the enemy a "Thief."

Chapter 10

WHY WERE ALL KILLED?

Knowing our Father is a Loving God – for the Word says: in 1John 4:8-10:

> *Whoever does not love does not know God, because **God is love**. **This** is how God showed his love among us: He sent his one and only Son into the world that we might live through him. This is love: **not** that we loved God, **but** that he loved us and sent his Son as an atoning sacrifice for our sins. (**emphasis mine**)*

When we read in Old Testament and foretold in coming days in the book of Revelation, of His requiring *all* to be killed, it can *seem* to not line up with the revelation of His love.

Until we look further.

In Old Testament times God required His people to destroy, "both man *and* beast" in a land, because that land had become overcome by the offspring of Fallen Angel engineered Giants, Nephilim, and chimera. The Fallen Angels had corrupted creation to the point where DNA was no longer the DNA created by our Creator. All of Creation had become the mixture of various species, as well as the mingling of Fallen Angel DNA and human DNA. The results were a distortion of the original, a corruption of God's original design.

He called for their destruction in His Mercy, in His attempt to try to restore mankind to its' original intent and purpose of relationship with each other and their Creator. When His people went into a land occupied by these mutants, He required the destruction of *every* semblance of the distortion of creation by the enemy's enticements and the sharing of information from the Tree of the Knowledge of Good and Evil.

These beings populated the earth and were intent on bringing corruption both before and, according to historical evidence, *after* the flood. Nimrod had tapped into the genetic manipulation made known by the fallen Watcher Angels and was in process of propagating it once again when God intervened and separated the languages of the peoples and scattered them. Each now had *some* of the knowledge but they could no longer work "as one man", God Himself said, "nothing would be impossible to them," and that was *after* the flood.

Those scattered at the time of Nimrod went throughout the earth. As the Hebrews began taking the land and cleansing it, there were some from locations, such as "The Valley of the Giants" southwest of Jerusalem, who escaped and traveled to distant lands carrying their corruption throughout the earth.

Today, we see depictions of just a few of these distortions of creation on the walls of caves and Pyramids around the world.

Below is a list of the major cultures with a history of these glyphs on the walls of caves, mounds or Pyramids showing similar creatures:

- Sumarians
- Babylonians
- Egyptians
- Phoenicians
- India
- Chinese
- Japanese
- Tibetian
- Greeks
- Romans
- Aztec
- Myans
- Incas
- Native American Tribes

"Myths" told around the world, in every long-standing culture, who have no record of an awareness of each other, tell of giant, six-toed, six-fingered, red-haired beings. Beings who were cannibalistic and homosexual, with vile, fierce features. These beings demanded to be served and worshipped. They became the Kings, the Tribal Leaders, the Chieftains requiring absolute obedience from the servile populations. They were believed to have "descended from the gods." These cultures all have stories also of small, winged creatures – some called "Fairies", and

"Gnomes" or "Jinn" – all distortions and results of genetic manipulation.

All of these cultures have a Creation story followed by "gods" who came out of the sky to cohabit with their women in exchange for "secrets". They all tell of generations of tyranny and advanced abilities until there came a flood! *All* of the above mentioned cultures tell of a great flood. And, all of these cultures have what we call "myths" telling of again after the flood being seduced to gain "knowledge" of creation. All have "Megaliths", prehistoric, *pre-flood* structures constructed of immense stones. These structures show cleanly cut circular holes through them which could *only* be made using some kind of machine.

Scientists to this day are puzzled as to the origin of these perfectly bored holes.[1] Not wanting to believe the veracity of scripture which tells of Fallen Angels with angelic knowledge coming to exchange this knowledge with mankind, these Archeologists are left with no explanation for what their eyes see.

Many have assumed the native cultures somehow managed to machine perfect bore holes, through several feet of granite, using stone chisels, leaving no chisel marks. Many Archeologists believe the natives moved these seventy to one-hundred ton foundation stones using ropes and pulleys – leaving no rope markings as are found in those locations where it is verified ropes were used. These Archeologists' say these indigenous farmers used a *lot* of man-power - they would have needed *thousands* around each stone, as these stones are proven to have been quarried from over twenty miles away in some cases! In Peru for instance, these megalith stones were moved over high mountain ranges, across rivers, through the valleys and back up high mountain peaks to become the foundation stones of Temples to these "gods".

On the Island of Sardinia, off the Coast of Italy, over 30,000 tombs of such Beings have recently been discovered. To this day the culture of the Island dictates boys, at the age of 13, be locked overnight in the entrance of one of these Tombs, to "gain power and strength" from the bones of the giant entombed within. Explorers with instrumentation have gone into some of the Tombs to discover, in fact, there is some kind of impulse being emitted, which do not show up outside of the Tomb. Scientists are trying to understand what this phenomenon could be. The DNA of Fallen Angel fathers, created to live eternally, with a life-force still being emitted? Through generations of cross-breeding these beings have been reduced in height, rather than the "height of Cedars" recorded in scripture.

Today, mankind are still trying to find ways to create giants.

> *GIANT: Genetic Investigation of Anthropometric Traits*
> *The **Genetic Investigation of Anthropometric Traits** (**GIANT**) consortium is an international collaboration that seeks to identify genetic loci that modulate human body size and shape, including height and measures of obesity. The GIANT consortium is a collaboration between investigators from many different groups, institutions, countries, and studies, and the results represent their combined efforts. The primary approach has been meta-analysis of genome-wide association data and other large-*

scale genetic data sets. Anthropometric traits that have been studied by GIANT include body mass index (BMI), height, and traits related to waist circumference (such as waist-hip ratio adjusted for BMI, or WHRadjBMI). Thus far, the GIANT consortium has identified common genetic variants at hundreds of loci that are associated with anthropometric traits.
http://portals.broadinstitute.org/collaboration/giant/index. php/GIANT_consortium

Governments and their institutions involved in this research advertise their intentions as wanting to help those afflicted with the "gigantism" gene. However, a disproportionate amount of funding is going into this effort, when you consider only about 3 people out of every 1 million have some form of gigantism.[5] There are those in the Mystery Religions and Occult funding an attempt to isolate this gene for their own uses.

Why the "Disinformation?"

Logic and rational reasoning is ignored as Scientists and Archeologists look at the writings, and spoken tradition of these cultures. "Politically Correct" Scientists and Archeologists ignore the histories of these cultures which deny having created these Megaliths, and instead tell of giant beings who ruled their people and created these structures. But, if they were to be believed, then we would have to believe the Bible and *not* accept the demonically inspired Darwinian Theory of evolution.

Mankind is being prepared, even by the Pope, to receive and believe that Extra-terrestrials are, in fact, our creators rather than the truth of the Bible. Almost daily we are hearing of the veracity of "extra-terrestrials". These are *not* extra-*terrestrials*, they *are* extra-*dimensional* demonic entities. We are daily being prepared, to receive these "Star Visitors, who seeded us millions of years ago and are now returning to help us." All part of the Luciferian Strategy to capture as much of mankind as possible.

Meanwhile, the Church, who is *supposed* to be the Ambassador of the Kingdom of Heaven, speaking the Truth to the nations, is speaking a watered-down feel-good gospel. Rather than take on difficult, *current* truth, it has taken on a defensive voice. Much of the Church is *reacting* rather than leading.

Using the method of "Gradualism" which *gradually* introduces an idea, the enemy began years ago to introduce his ideas. LGBT for instance, when first mentioned was received by the masses as reprehensible. But, the enemy, through his agents and the ignorant used the principle of Gradualism to present a "what if" idea: "What *if* a person is *born* with a sexual orientation?" then "What *if* two people fall in love, are we to deny them LOVE just because they're of the same sex according to *our* definition?" As these ideas found discussion and became more and more publicized, using the enemy's controlled Media and the unlearned and innocent, as well as those who are knowing participants of the enemy's agenda, these enemy inspired ideas become common place. God made a Decree against this lifestyle because He *knows* how He created our bodies to function. He knows the diseases this lifestyle generates, both physical as well as spiritual and emotional.

He knows He created us to *procreate*, which is the primary reason the enemy so promotes this lifestyle, contrary to our Creators purpose to *procreate* us, our enemy's purpose is to *exterminate* us.

Much of the Church, rather than unapologetically speaking the Truth to these lies, has become "tolerant" and "inclusive", thereby *including* and becoming *tolerant* of lifestyles Decreed as reprehensible by the God who created us. Much of the Church has thereby included and become tolerant of sin as acceptable. In taking this stance, much of the Church has made the Cross of Christ unnecessary, the Blood of Jesus, shed to cleanse us from sin, is no longer necessary according to this new "gospel". If there is no sin, if rather, there is an excuse, if a person "can't help" their behavior" then cleansing is not necessary. The uncomfortable step of recognizing and acknowledging our sin before a Holy God is eliminated. The immense sense of Freedom and cleansing experienced by those of us who have made this step, the sense of surrender to He Who is our Creator and Father, is missed. Without this step, this experiential encounter, mankind becomes their own god, making their own laws. There are no Moral Absolutes, now, "whatever makes us feel good is right." Many unwittingly have accepted this "gospel." Others, due to their Pride and Rebellion, have found this "gospel", this belief, more to their liking, they don't *want* to know the Truth, because it would mean their giving up what they *like*. It would mean *surrendering* to someone Greater than themselves. They are not willing to even *entertain* such an idea! There are millions of adherents of this "gospel" who *knowingly* serve these demonic entities, hoping "it'll all work out in the end". Many have given themselves over to the lies, willingly surrendering and giving themselves over to the enemy – ironically – taking the very step they so abhor, that kept them from surrendering to the Creator their will. All who have accepted these ideas have accepted the demonic inspiration of the evil spirits of the offspring of the Fallen Angels, who sit and laugh delightedly as they mock both mankind and their Creator.

Chapter 11

WHY WE CARE

There are many good, sound Resources available, which I've listed in the back of this work, to enable you to do your own research and see the findings for yourself.

But, why do we care? IF all of this is true, why do we, today, care? Why are we, as Christians, looking into this information? Why do we care if there were giants or fallen angels?

First, we care for Truths sake. We care because the distortion and perversion of Creation has not stopped. We care because if we are not aware of the schemes of the enemy, if we ignore him, as past generations have, then we empower him.

If information points to the Bible's narrative as being accurate, the Elitist don't want it propagated. If it goes against Darwinian evolution, it's not to be spoken. Professors, Archeologists' and others have lost their tenure and positions for daring to speak the truth.

We care because to sit at ease in our lives, caught up with the affairs of this life only as it regards us, blinds us to the scheme of things around us. Our Father God is moving Heaven and Earth to try to get Truth to earths' inhabitants, but many ignore the Truth because it makes them uncomfortable. Then, suddenly, seemingly without warning, disaster strikes. The following scripture in Amos speaks to

this mindset.

Amos 6:1-7 (NLT)

What sorrow awaits you who lounge in luxury in Jerusalem, and you who feel secure in Samaria! You are famous and popular in Israel, and people go to you for help. But go over to Calneh and see what happened there. Then go to the great city of Hamath and down to the Philistine city of Gath. You are no better than they were, and look at how they were destroyed. You push away every thought of coming disaster, but your actions only bring the day of judgment closer. How terrible for you who sprawl on ivory beds and lounge on your couches, eating the meat of tender lambs from the flock and of choice calves fattened in the stall. You sing trivial songs to the sound of the harp and fancy yourselves to be great musicians like David. You drink wine by the bowlful and perfume yourselves with fragrant lotions. You care nothing about the ruin of your nation. Therefore, you will be the first to be led away as captives. Suddenly, all your parties will end.

This scripture was speaking to Israel at the time, but the same mindset is prevalent today in mankind.

We care because we were given forewarning when Jesus said:

Matthew 24:37-39 New Life Version (NLV)

"When the Son of Man comes, it will be the same as when Noah lived. In the days before the flood, people were eating and drinking. They were marrying and being given in

marriage. This kept on until the day Noah went into the large boat. They did not know what was happening until the flood came and the water carried them all away. It will be like this when the Son of Man comes.

We've looked at the condition of the earth in the days of Noah when Fallen Angels were ruling as gods and their offspring were ravaging mankind. When Fallen Angels were exchanging the Knowledge of Good and Evil with mankind in exchange for servitude.

We are warned:

Ecclesiastes 1:9-11 (KJV)

The thing that hath been, it is that which shall be; and that which is done is that which shall be done: and there is no new thing under the sun. Is there anything whereof it may be said, See, this is new? it hath been already of old time, which was before us. There is no remembrance of former things; neither shall there be any remembrance of things that are to come with those that shall come after.

We care because we don't have to fall subservient to this scheme. We *can* be equipped to "resist the enemy and he *will* flee." Jesus Himself said, when the seventy returned whom He had sent enemy in His day:

Luke 10:17-20 (KJV)

And the seventy returned again with joy, saying, Lord, even the devils are subject unto us through thy name. And he said unto them, I beheld Satan as lightning fall from heaven. Behold, I give unto you power to tread on serpents and scorpions, and over all the power of the enemy: and nothing shall by any means hurt you. (emphasis mine). Notwithstanding in this rejoice not, that the spirits are subject unto you; but rather rejoice, because your names are written in heaven.

Understanding "serpents and scorpions" were metaphors for various types of the enemy, we can see Jesus never intended His own to be the hapless victim of the enemy. Yes, there are those called to Martyrdom, but for the rest of us, we are to exercise the Authority bequeathed to us. Understand, that just as our Government cannot give Military grade weapons to untrained, uncommitted civilians, neither can our Father God entrust His Authority and weaponry to those who are not in submission to Him. The seven sons of Sceva learned this lesson:

Acts 19:13-16 (ASV) But certain also of the strolling Jews, exorcists, took upon them to name over them that had the evil spirits the name of the Lord Jesus, saying, I adjure you by Jesus whom Paul preacheth. And there were seven sons of one Sceva, a Jew, a chief priest, who did this. And the evil spirit answered and said unto them, Jesus I know, and Paul I know, but who are ye? And the man in whom the evil spirit was leaped on them, and mastered both of them, and prevailed against them, so that they fled out of that house naked and wounded.

Our position is based upon our relationship. It's not a matter of "favoritism", it's a matter of the heart of surrender. Just as Shadrach, Meshach and Abednego declared centuries ago: in *Daniel 3:16-18:*

> *Shadrach, Meshach and Abednego replied to him, "King Nebuchadnezzar, we do not need to defend ourselves before you in this matter. If we are thrown into the blazing furnace, the God we serve is able to deliver us from it, and he will deliver us from Your Majesty's hand. **But** even if he does not, we want you to know, Your Majesty, that we will not serve your gods or worship the image of gold you have set up."(**emphasis mine**)*

We see from this that they fully *knew* God was *able* to deliver them, and ultimately *would* deliver them from the Kings' hand – even if that meant in death, they *knew* they were not given over to this King. Even if they were to be devoured by the flames, it would not alter their relationship with their God. And, after a night of walking in the fire with them, God was able to save them from the fiery furnace.

So many base their relationship with God on their circumstances. If they go through tragedy and difficulty and they pray and the difficulty does not go away, they walk away from the Lord and choose to believe either He doesn't care or doesn't exist. Their relationship is circumstantial, where as our Fathers' relationship with us says, "I will *never* leave you, nor will I *ever* forsake you." Just as in a marriage we vow to one another, "for better or for worse, in sickness or in health..." there's *commitment* – without which we have a one-sided "relationship." We cannot fully participate in all of the aspects of a relationship with God if we are in a "conditional" relationship which says, "Well, I'll believe if You do such and such or so and forth..." or "I *did* believe until..." Faith, Believing, isn't a matter of just believing God is and Jesus is His Son – scripture tells us even demons believe this – because they *do* know the Truth – remember the enemy in the wilderness tempting Jesus with scripture? He said in James 2:19-20(AVS)

> *Thou believest that God is one; thou doest well: the demons also believe, and shudder.* [20] *But wilt thou know, O vain man, that faith apart from works is barren?*

He *knew* scripture – it's not a matter of *knowing* it's a matter of *submitting* to the Truth. It's a matter of knowing to the point it doesn't matter how that truth is lived out in your life, you still believe God to be Who He says He is, and Who He has shown Himself to be at the Cross of Christ. At Calvary God *demonstrated* and proved His love to mankind by so greatly loving and dearly prizing the world that He *gave* His only Son. No one extracted or demanded that giving, God knew it was the *only* way to bring mankind back into relationship with Himself and so He voluntarily gave.

There are many today in various Doctrines who have given away much of their Authority over the enemy. They believe and are in relationship with the Father, and when they die will be with Him, but while here on earth they have relinquished much of their Authority over sickness and the enemy's attacks. As long as we draw breath we need to be pressing in to know more of this unfathomable God!

God has forewarned us of the realities of the "Last Days", but we are challenged to believe what He has said. When "sudden destruction" comes upon the earth, where even "the very elect will be deceived" we are challenged to be prepared.

We care about the truths of history and their relevance to today, because we want to be trained and equipped so that we don't have this sudden destruction fall upon us unawares.

It has been said: "He who controls History determines the Future." The Luciferian Strategy as lived out through his agents is to hide and distort true History so they can determine our Future, however, the Truth is, we *can* "occupy until Jesus returns". We *can* live and move and have our being living with all Authority over *all* the works of the enemy – and *nothing* shall by any means harm us. We are *not* to live in fear of the enemy and what He *is* bringing on this earth. We can live in total confidence, as Shadrach, Meshach and Abednego did, that our God *is* able and will deliver us. Yes, they spent a night in a fiery furnace, I can only imagine the experience, but they were not alone, and neither will those of us be who live in the last days.

The Luciferian Strategy

Chapter 12

THE BOOK OF REVELATION

Now, looking at the Book of Revelation and the coming days, we have to ask, why does God once again call for the total destruction of every man, woman or child as recorded in the Old Testament? In the future those being destroyed will be those receiving "the mark of the beast".

Why would a loving Father, who is so readily available to all who call upon Him in truth, who has so clearly demonstrated His willingness to forgive, not forgive any who receive, "the mark of the beast"?

What did Jesus mean when He said: in *Matthew 24:36-39 (ASV)*

> *But of that day and hour knoweth no one, not even the angels of heaven, neither the Son, but the Father only. And **as were the days of Noah, so shall be the coming of the Son of man.** For as in those days which were before the flood they were eating and drinking, marrying and giving in marriage, until the day that Noah entered into the ark, and they knew not until the flood came, and took them all away; so shall be the coming of the Son of man. (**emphasis mine**)*

We looked earlier at the condition of the earth, "in the days of Noah." We noted the meaning of Noah's "perfection" not being a perfection of *action*, but a perfection of *being*.

Noah and his family were the only ones on earth who's DNA had not been corrupted.

The life the Fallen Angels had created on earth was going on as it had for generations.

Let's look at the approximate timeline of those events to get a clearer understanding of the Twelve-hundred (1200) years these fallen angels had to corrupt the entire earth.

The Book of Enoch chapter 6 tells us:

> *And it came to pass when the children of men had multiplied that in those days were born unto them beautiful and comely daughters. And the angels, the children of the heaven, saw and lusted after them, and said to one another: 'Come, let us choose us wives from among the children of men and beget us children.' And Semjâzâ, who was their leader, said unto them: 'I fear ye will not indeed agree to do this deed, and I alone shall have to pay the penalty of a great sin.' And they all answered him and said: 'Let us all swear an oath, and all bind ourselves by mutual imprecations not to abandon this plan but to do this thing.' Then sware they all together and bound themselves by mutual imprecations upon it. And they were in all two hundred; who descended ⌐ in the*

days 7 of Jared on the summit of Mount Hermon, and they called it Mount Hermon, because they had sworn and bound themselves by mutual imprecations upon it.

Remember the name "Hermon" in Hebrew means "Anathema" or "devoted to destruction".

Jared lived to be nine-hundred and sixty-two according to biblical timelines, somewhere in that timeline the Watcher Angels "left their first estate" and spent the next thousand years or so overtly corrupting Creation, until the Father sent the flood to cleanse Creation.

Here's a timeline from the time of Adam to the Flood.

Event/Person	Passage	Total Time (in years)
God created everything.	*Genesis 1–2*	0
Adam became the father of Seth at 130.	*Genesis 5:3*	0 + 130 = 130
Seth became the father of Enosh at 105.	*Genesis 5:6*	130 + 105 = 235
Enosh became the father of Kenan at 90.	*Genesis 5:9*	235 + 90 = 325

Cainan became the father of Mahalalel at 70.	*Genesis 5:12*	325 + 70 = 395
Mahalalel became the father of Jared at 65.	*Genesis 5:15*	395 + 65 = 460
Jared became the father of Enoch at 162.	*Genesis 5:18*	460 + 162 = 622
Enoch became the father of Methuselah at 65.	*Genesis 5:21*	622 + 65 = 687
Methuselah became the father of Lamech at 187.	*Genesis 5:25*	687 + 187 = 874
Lamech became the father of Noah at 182.	*Genesis 5:28*	874 + 182 = 1056
The Flood started when Noah was 600.	*Genesis 7:6*	1056 + 600 = 1656

Jared fathered Enoch at 162, so we can safely assume *sometime* before that, the Watcher Angels made their unholy pact and descended on Mt. Hermon to begin their quest to take over creation. Jared fathered Enoch sometime around the year 622 and the Flood came in the year 1656 – therefore, *conservatively* speaking these Fallen Angels had twelve-hundred years (1200) to spread their corruption and The Tree of the Knowledge of Good and Evil technology throughout the earth. Twelve-hundred years ago from the year twenty-seventeen is the year eight-seventeen. Think of the advances, the events that have taken place since the year 817 AD. Imagine then that amount of time occupied by angelic beings populating the earth with advanced angelic technology available to them. What would technology look like today?

Evolutionists would have us believe that those living at that time were all a bunch of ignorant Cavemen. It fits their narrative to use all of their resources, financed by the Occultist's and Mystery Religions, to have us believe we "evolved" from these "primates". The Truth, if we will simply believe what our eyes *see*, is that the pre-flood inhabitants of the entire earth – not just what we now call the Middle East, were an extremely advanced population. Many of the things found *around the earth* are so advanced. Scientists today *still* have no explanation for their existence. Megalith structures are just *one* example. Esoteric knowledge was widely accessed and utilized. Interesting we, as Christians, believe and delight in retelling of Jesus "suddenly appearing in their midst" in the upper room. We delight in the Apostles "finding themselves" in another location. We marvel at Jesus commanding the storm "peace be still" and it obeys. We marvel at "the handkerchief of Paul" being used to convey healing. The shadow of Peter bringing healing. How? We think *only* Jesus and His Disciples had these abilities. But, many of Jesus' followers today experience these same phenomena. There are elements in Creation itself that we have tapped into without even understanding the dynamics. *We*, those of us in relationship with the Father through Jesus, access these dynamics through "Faith". The Occultists access these dynamics through an understanding of the dynamics of Creation.

What *is* "Faith"? Scripture tells us: in *Hebrews 11:1-40 (ASV)* *Now faith is assurance of things hoped for, a conviction of things not seen. For therein the elders had witness borne to them. By faith we understand that the worlds have been framed by the word of God, so that what is seen hath not been made out of things which appear. By faith Abel offered unto God a more excellent sacrifice than Cain, through which he had witness borne to him that he was righteous, God bearing witness in respect of his gifts: and through it he being dead yet speaketh. By faith Enoch was translated that he should not see death; and he was not found, because God translated him: for he hath had witness borne to him that before his translation he had been well-pleasing unto God: And without faith it is impossible to be well-pleasing unto him; for he that cometh to God must believe that he is, and that he is a rewarder of them that seek after him. By faith Noah, being warned of God concerning things not seen as yet, moved with godly fear, prepared an ark to the saving of his house; through which he condemned the world, and became heir of the righteousness which is according to faith. By faith Abraham, when he was called, obeyed to go out unto a place which he was to receive for an inheritance; and he went out, not knowing whither he went. By faith he became a sojourner in the land of promise, as in a land not his own, dwelling in tents, with Isaac and Jacob, the heirs with him of the same promise: for he looked for the city which hath the foundations, whose builder and maker is God. By faith even Sarah herself received power to conceive seed when she was past age, since she counted him faithful who had promised: wherefore also there sprang of one, and him as*

1

good as dead, so many as the stars of heaven in multitude, and as the sand, which is by the sea-shore, innumerable. These all died in faith, not having received the promises, but having seen them and greeted them from afar, and having confessed that they were strangers and pilgrims on the earth. For they that say such things make it manifest that they are seeking after a country of their own. And if indeed they had been mindful of that country from which they went out, they would have had opportunity to return. But now they desire a better country, that is, a heavenly: wherefore God is not ashamed of them, to be called their God; for he hath prepared for them a city. By faith Abraham, being tried, offered up Isaac: yea, he that had gladly received the promises was offering up his only begotten son; even he to whom it was said, In Isaac shall thy seed be called: accounting that God is able to raise up, even from the dead; from whence he did also in a figure receive him back. By faith Isaac blessed Jacob and Esau, even concerning things to come. By faith Jacob, when he was dying, blessed each of the sons of Joseph; and worshipped, leaning upon the top of his staff. By faith Joseph, when his end was nigh, made mention of the departure of the children of Israel; and gave commandment concerning his bones. By faith Moses, when he was born, was hid three months by his parents, because they saw he was a goodly child; and they were not afraid of the king's commandment. By faith Moses, when he was grown up, refused to be called the son of Pharaoh's daughter; choosing rather to share ill treatment with the people of God, than to enjoy the pleasures of sin for a season; accounting the reproach of Christ greater riches than the treasures of Egypt: for he looked unto the recompense of reward. By faith he forsook Egypt, not fearing the wrath of the king: for he endured, as seeing him who is invisible. By faith he kept the passover, and the sprinkling of the blood, that the destroyer of the firstborn should not touch them. By faith they passed through the Red sea as by dry land: which the Egyptians assaying to do were swallowed up. By faith the walls of Jericho fell down, after they had been compassed about for seven days. By faith Rahab the harlot perished not with them that were disobedient, having received the spies with peace. And what shall I more say? for the time will fail me if I tell of Gideon, Barak, Samson, Jephthah; of David and Samuel and the prophets: who through faith subdued kingdoms, wrought righteousness, obtained promises, stopped the mouths of lions, quenched the power of fire, escaped the edge of the sword, from weakness were made strong, waxed mighty in war, turned to flight armies of aliens. Women received their dead by a resurrection: and others were tortured, not accepting their deliverance that they might obtain a better resurrection: and others had trial of mockings and scourgings, yea, moreover of bonds and imprisonment: they were stoned, they were sawn asunder, they were tempted, they were slain with the sword: they went about in sheepskins, in goatskins; being destitute, afflicted, ill-treated (of whom the world was not worthy), wandering in deserts and mountains and caves, and the holes of the earth. And these all, having had witness borne to them through their faith, received not the promise, God having provided some better thing concerning us, that apart from us they should not be made perfect.

The word "assurance" used in verse one, is sometimes translated "conviction" or "substance". This word comes from the Greek hupostasis (Strong's # 5287), which means "a placing or setting under, a substructure or foundation." This word appears elsewhere in the New Testament as "confident" or "confidence" (2 Corinthians 9:4; 11:17; Hebrews 3:14).

Which "Confidence" we will have when we are in *relationship* with the Creator. When we *know* Him and *communicate* with Him and not just have a nodding acquaintance with Him, we will have this *confidence* – this "Faith" that what He says is True. Verse three says, by faith we believe:
By faith we understand that the worlds have been framed by the word of God, so that what is seen hath not been made out of things which appear.

We *believe,* because we *know* - we *know* our Father and we know Who He is. When the "Scientists" of the world try to convince us of their distortions, we look to the Word and see the Truth. The Scientists' who look and see and *believe* what their eyes tell them are scoffed and mocked and dismissed, while the Evolutionists' distortions are displayed and taught to young, vulnerable minds as truth.

Interesting, just *one* aspect of the Evolutionists doctrine to look at, they say mankind evolved from a one-cell thing, up and up and up to ape-like then upright then homo-sapiens. True science questions this theory on the basis that, if that *theory* were true, mankind would be the *only* instance where you see this kind of evolution UP...*every* other instance, when something is left to its' own devices, it *degenerates*. And, excuse my asking, but, even if that convoluted theory *were* true - WHO created the first cell?

I can look in my refrigerator after a week and see *that* principle of degeneration in operation! But we are told not to believe what we *see,* believe what we are told. We *see* megalithic structures *around the world* that have *obviously* gone through a devastating flood, as evidenced by the way they are tossed about and embedded with sea shells – on top of thousands of feet high mountain tops. We see locations *around the world* that are in *perfect* astronomical alignment with the Constellations and the Solstices and lunar cycles, and we're told to believe these were *accidentally* aligned by cavemen-like natives of that particular land OR somehow observed by the farmers of the land and then created to help their farming. We ignore huge giant skulls, large enough to fit easily over the head of a man, found *around the world* and believe them to be an aberration.

We read of giants in scripture – and are told they existed *after* flood, but that's an inconvenient truth, it doesn't fit our "belief system," so we exchange the truth for a lie. We read of healing that took place in the New Testament and again, it doesn't fit in our "belief system," so we deny it's Truth. In doing so we open ourselves up for deception, believing the same lie the enemy enticed Eve with, "Hath God said?" Our answer should be a resounding, "YES! Now, Lord, teach me please! I see it in your Word but I don't *believe* it!" We would be better served for these days, to come before the Father with an attitude of, "there's more to this Universe and You as an Unfathomable God, then I am aware, please, teach me Truth."

The enemy for his part is meanwhile busy revealing mysteries of the universe to his followers and enticing them so as to capture them for his use.

Creation is an obedient servant, submitted to whoever exercises Authority over it. If we, as the *Legitimate* Overseer abandon our post, and leave Creation to the agents of the enemy, then Creation is captured by them and the strength and anointing it has, is hijacked. Romans 8:19-21 confirms this:

> *For the creation waits in eager expectation for the children of God to be revealed. For the creation was subjected to frustration, not by its own choice, but by the will of the one who subjected it, in hope that the creation itself will be liberated from its bondage to decay and brought into the freedom and glory of the children of God.*

Creation *groans* waiting for us! Meanwhile, as servants, they obey those who come to them speaking the language of scripture – even though it is *distorted.*

Let me illustrate: when Lucifer enticed Eve, he spoke truth, but it wasn't the *whole* truth. When he told Eve, "You shall not surely die." He *knew* God was speaking of *total* death. But being cunning he spoke *only* of the death of the *body.* "You shall not surely die." Eve, enticed, ate and *behold* she did *not* immediately die – not the death of her physical body, but death now entered her DNA and her body began it's physical decay, meanwhile her spirit died instantly with that first bite. She no longer saw herself as God created her to be, she no longer enjoyed her fellowship with her Father the Creator, rather she and then Adam after, succumbed to the enticement and hid from their Father. Jesus in the wilderness, when tempted by the enemy, was enticed with half-truths, the *letter of the word, without the Spirit of the Word.* But Jesus, as man, *knew* His Father God, He knew, not just the *letter* of the Word, but the *Spirit* of the Word. He was in relationship with the Holy Spirit and *knew* Him, and in knowing Him, He knew the fullness of the Word.

Luke 4:1-13 confirms this:
Jesus, full of the Holy Spirit, left the Jordan and was led by the Spirit into the wilderness, where for forty days he was tempted by the devil. He ate nothing during those days, and at the end of them he was hungry. The devil said to him, "If you are the Son of God, tell this stone to become bread." Jesus answered, "It is written: 'Man shall not live on bread alone." The devil led him up to a high place and showed him in an instant all the kingdoms of the world. And he said to him, "I will give you all their authority and splendor; it has been given to me, and I can give it to anyone I want to. If you worship me, it will all be yours." Jesus answered, "It is written: 'Worship the Lord your God and serve him only.'" The devil led him to Jerusalem and had him stand on the highest point of the temple. "If you are the Son of God," he said, "throw yourself down from here. For it is written: " 'He will command his angels concerning you to guard you carefully; they will lift you up in their hands, so that you will

not strike your foot against a stone.' " Jesus answered, "It is said: 'Do not put the Lord your God to the test.' " When the devil had finished all this tempting, he left him.

We see here how intimately the enemy *knows* Creation, he *knows* not only how we were created and formed, but all of Creation. He was with the Father in the beginning, he watched and learned, and unfortunately, unlike the Holy Angels that *rejoiced* seeing Creation coming to pass, he grew jealous. *until an opportune time.* He was assigned as the Commander of the Watcher Angels, to watch over Creation, which he obviously did for a time. In his watching the Father coming into the Garden each evening to commune with Adam, and watching as Adam worked as a *partner* with God in naming Creation, he grew jealous. He then agreed with that jealousy until he determined *he* would be as God.

The Occultists access Fallen Angel technology and Esoteric knowledge through incantations which communicate with the spirits of the offspring of these Fallen Angels, who *understand* DNA, which *we* have only recently *begun* to understand. These demonic beings understand the dynamics of Creation, and are willing to share it with those who will exchange their souls for this knowledge. Meanwhile, we, the ones all of Creation was created for, run in fear of such knowledge because the enemy has convinced us it's "New Age" it's "Demonic", which it is as it is used by them. He *knows* we are Sealed in Jesus and he has no access to us, the best he can do is to keep us from *knowing* who we are in Jesus. He lies to keep us from believing healing is for today, "Who do you think you are? He questions us. ONLY Apostles could heal! That was for THEN not for today." He deceives us to believe we are at the whim of Creation, there's nothing we can do about storms or corruption in the earth. "It's the End of Days, scripture tells us these things are going to come to pass – there's nothing we can do!"

Luke 10:19-20, states this clearly:-

I have given you authority to trample on snakes and scorpions and to overcome all the power of the enemy; nothing will harm you. However, do not rejoice that the spirits submit to you, but rejoice that your names are written in heaven.

I *have* to ask, why would Jesus give us ALL Authority over ALL the works of the enemy – and NOTHING by ANY means shall harm us – if we aren't supposed to *use* that Authority? Rather, I believe our challenge is to learn *how* to use that Authority in submission to HIS Authority. Just as a good General is in full submission to his Commander in Chief.

Also in Ephesians 6: 10-20, Paul states:-

*Finally, be strong in the Lord and in his mighty power. Put on the full armor of God, so that you can take your stand against the devil's schemes. For our struggle is not against flesh and blood, but against the rulers, against the authorities, against the powers of this dark world and against the spiritual forces of evil in the heavenly realms. **Therefore put on the full armor of God,** so that when the day of evil comes, you may be able to stand your ground, and after you have done everything, to stand. Stand firm then, with the belt of truth buckled around your waist, with the breastplate of* *righteousness in place, and with your feet fitted with the readiness that comes from the gospel of peace. In addition to all this, take up the shield of faith, with which you can extinguish all the flaming arrows of the evil one. Take the helmet of salvation and the sword of the Spirit, which is the word of God. (**emphasis mine**)*

And pray in the Spirit on all occasions with all kinds of prayers and requests. With this in mind, be alert and always keep on praying for all the Lord's people. Pray also for me, that whenever I speak, words may be given me so that I will fearlessly make known the mystery of the gospel, for which I am an ambassador in chains. Pray that I may declare it fearlessly, as I should.

Just *two* of numerous scriptures. If we were to wait passively for Him to Rapture us out of this earth, the Father would not have given us Armor. If we are to sit passively in our pews, He wouldn't have spent so much of scripture telling us of our gifts and our abilities in Him. He would not have given us a Sword, which is the Word of God, if we were not to *use* it.

Meanwhile, the enemy equips his followers to steal the powers of Creation and uses them to corrupt not only mankind but all of Creation. When we, the true Overseers *should* and *could* be speaking into Creation to submit themselves to the Living Word and VOMIT every evil incantation, every wicked enchantment. Remember, Creation is *groaning* waiting for the Redeemed, the Sons of God, to function as Sons and set Creation free, just as Jesus did when He spoke to the storm and said "Peace, be still."

Psalm 148 says:

> *Praise the Lord.*
> *Praise the Lord from the heavens;*
> *praise him in the heights above.*
> *Praise him, all his angels;*
> *praise him, all his heavenly hosts.*
> *Praise him, sun and moon;*
> *praise him, all you shining stars.*
> *Praise him, you highest heavens*
> *and you waters above the skies.*
> *Let them praise the name of the Lord,*
> *for at his command they were created,*
> *and he established them for ever and ever—*
> *he issued a decree that will never pass away.*
> *Praise the Lord from the earth,*
> *you great sea creatures and all ocean depths,*
> *lightning and hail, snow and clouds,*
> ***stormy winds that do his bidding,***
> *you mountains and all hills,*
> *fruit trees and all cedars,*
> *wild animals and all cattle,*
> *small creatures and flying birds,*
> *kings of the earth and all nations,*
> *you princes and all rulers on earth,*
> *young men and women,*
> *old men and children.*
> *Let them praise the name of the Lord,*
> *for his name alone is exalted;*
> *his splendor is above the earth and the heavens.*

> *And he has raised up for his people a horn,*
> *the praise of all his faithful servants,*
> *of Israel, the people close to his heart.*
> **(emphasis mine)**

Just looking at verse eight, we can see that stormy winds are to "obey HIS bidding" – our Father's bidding – not Occultists', who speak incantations into the heavens and call for devastating, destructive storms. There's power, strength, Authority in Agreement.

> Matthew 18:19-20 *"Again, truly I tell you that if two of you on earth agree about anything they ask for, it will be done for them by my Father in heaven. For where two or three gather in my name, there am I with them."*

The terminology of "gathering in my name" when studied out, will show there's an agreement with HIM, His nature, His Will – remember the story of the Apostles as they left a town that did not receive them, they asked Jesus: "Shall we call down fire to destroy them?"

> **Luke 9:54-56 (KJV)**
> *And when his disciples James and John saw this, they said, Lord, wilt thou that we command fire to come down from heaven, and consume them, even as Elias did? But he turned, and rebuked them, and said, Ye know not what manner of spirit ye are of. For the Son of man is not come to destroy men's lives, but to save them. And they went to another village.*

Just a side-note here...note, they didn't question *if* they had the *ability* to call down fire, they questioned if they *should*. When we "pray in agreement", when we gather for "prayer", we don't just gather willy-nilly and agree together for a pink Cadillac without asking if that's HIS Will for the situation! Again – *relationship* – submission to HIS Will and *Ways*. As in the above scripture, calling down fire to destroy those that didn't agree with Him was not in alignment and agreement with His *Ways*. So, when we, His Representatives here on earth, speak into Creation in Agreement with His Will, Creation *gladly* obeys! They – ALL of Creation, Sun, Moon Stars – ALL of Creation *groans* under the oppression of the Occultists and the sin of Adam, waiting for the revelation of the Sons of God to come and free them with the message of Redemption, the Blood of Jesus, the Cross of Christ, which freed us *and* Creation.

The Mantra of the Elitists and Occultists is: "As above so below." For those of us familiar with Scripture and "The Lord's Prayer" that concept sounds familiar. Jesus was asked by His Disciples to teach them to pray, in the book of Matthew 6:9, He answered saying, *"'This, then, is how you should pray:*

> *"'Our Father in heaven,*
> *hallowed be your name,*
> *your kingdom come,*
> *your will be done,*
> *on earth as it is in heaven.*
> *Give us today our daily bread.*
> *And forgive us our debts,*
> *as we also have forgiven our debtors.*

And lead us not into temptation,
but deliver us from the evil one. "

Here again, we see Lucifer wanting to be as God. He demands that his followers copy the Constellations and the heavens in Art and Architecture, with the Mantra, "As above so below," trying to imitate and thereby hoping to duplicate. The difference is, the Original is *always* more precious, more *real* than the copy. Precious things like diamonds, or the Heaven our Heavenly Father has prepared for us *cannot* be duplicated!

Chapter 13

WHERE WE ARE NOW

As we have seen, adherents of the "Mystery Religions", as Occult groups have been known through the ages, found individuals and causes to rally populations around. "Evolutionists" make up one of those strong advocate groups. Evolutionists began by thinking they were "advanced" in their thinking, they challenged everything society had been built upon until their time. They focused on, and specialized in, mocking and scorning the Bible and those who believed its' pages. At the time those who held true to the Bible did not have "scientific" knowledge to *prove* the Bible was true, it became a matter of faith alone.

Today, with the advances in true Science, the Bible is repeatedly being proven accurate. However, due to the generations of skepticism and the funding of the Elitist, institutions today have taken on the rhetoric of the Evolutionists and Occultists, as truth, teaching it as truth and "science." To disagree with the Doctrines of the controlling money financing these institutions and Foundations is to invite a loss of Tenure or Position. Thus, the Luciferian Agenda and its' adherents continue unabated. These Institutions of higher learning and groups behind the scenes controlling the purse strings of Governments and Corporations world-wide, are today running rampant with a systematic agenda. We hear of the "Globalist" agenda, those who would have us do away with National borders and National allegiance. "One-World Government" Adherents, who would have us believe we are all just one big community and have outgrown the days of individual Nations.

We now have a "World Court", where affairs are brought outside of National borders for the Judges sitting on the World Court to decide for a Nation. All of these appeal to our sense of "community" our "oneness" as a people. It all *looks* so idyllic, but behind this rhetoric is a sinister agenda to set societies up for A One World Ruler.

Today's Technology

While the Elitists introduce bright, shiny new toys for the populations to be distracted by, they work to bring about their centuries old, behind the scenes agenda.

Step by step, ancient Angelic knowledge is being introduced for acceptance. First we are systematically de-sensitized to the technology through "Sci-Fi" Movies. "Imaginations", ideas too incredible to ever be true...then, slowly we begin to hear a report here, a report there of "Science fiction" becoming real.

IOT

IOT (Internet of Things) advancement is on the horizon. THINGS "talk" to each other. Your alarm clock tells the coffee maker you are awake so it can begin making coffee. Your thermostat is set to know when you are awake and adjusts the temperature. Our new refrigerators can tell our phones when we're out of milk or other refrigerated items. The day is quickly coming when you will summon a driverless car via your smart phone, which will also tell it where you want to go and when – no more traffic jams! Where you live, what time you get up, what you eat, where you shop, where you spend your leisure time, how many are in your family and where you work, all stored on the Worldwide web...accessible information. All made possible by a series of low flying satellites and massive computers. The lure is ease of living, no more traffic jams, forgotten items on our shopping lists or appointments and available internet *worldwide*. No more "third-world country" blackouts.

Genetic Engineering:

"Genetic engineering" as first depicted in "science fiction" movies, is beginning to make newspaper mention. Cloning, once thought of as pure fiction, is now common place in laboratories. We're told its' use is generally for plants and animals, however it is acknowledged that there *are* Chimeras in Laboratories around the world. Acknowledging only God has the ability to breathe a Soul into existence is beyond the scope of this Science. The enticement of being able to "play God" silences consciences.

The lure of Technology:

Not long ago, families sat around the dinner table and exchanged information, victories and concerns from their day. Today, it is rare for a family to sit together and share a meal, and too often when they do, many are sharing their day on their phones, using Facebook or other "social media." In restaurants, it's common to see families sitting together with the children totally engrossed with their phones, resenting the intrusion of conversation. Like Lemmings depicted in "fiction", we march along in full agreement with the pretty, shiny things placed in our hands to keep us from seeing and facing reality and each other. These electronic "games" are many times designed to introduce the "powers" available to us, if only we say the right words or align ourselves with the "right" powers, we can have "magical Power." These "games" teach our children the names of these various entities. They teach killing isn't permanent. Dying isn't permanent. You can kill your enemy and in the next round – there he is again. Young minds just learning all concepts are learning they can die but not die, they come back in the next round. Reincarnation is the enemy's answer to true Redemption. Their lie is, we don't all die, we come back in the next life to fix the errors of this life. No need for true Redemption or forgiveness.

Cartoons

"Cartoons" have slowly evolved into introductions into the Occult and Occultic power. These entities, having hijacked the true powers of the Universe through the Tree of the Knowledge of Good and Evil, now delight in offending our Creator God by teaching mankind what they know will destroy them, by illegitimately acquiring this knowledge and misusing it. Cartoons today, introduce the concepts of magic, spells, enchantments and incantations.

All of which does *not* mean we don't use electronics, it simply means to be *aware* and *use* the electronics – don't become a slave to them, thereby allowing them to use you.

Stay alert to those around you. Stay connected to the humans around you, not just the electronics.

Separating mankind from each other and from our Father God is the enemy's delight. Separating us by any means, offense, distractions or lifestyle is not acceptable.

Talking to our Pets

A popular technology now being introduced, is the soon-coming ability to "talk to our pets."[11] Today in the U.S. its popular for families to have "fur babies," they used to be called "pets," cats and dogs, but now they are "fur babies." Animals, which in *many* countries around the world provide a staple of protein, in America have become children- substitutes. Think how much easier it is to have "fur babies" then children! No diaper changing, teething, tantrums or fears of independent behavior – just constant adoring and obedience! No need for *human* relationship or procreation.

Keeping us from procreating, as we were created to is just one goal. The hidden agenda of the Occultists' is to deceive and entice innocent victims, such as those deceived by the **LGBT** lifestyle, engaging them into a lifestyle which keeps them from procreating as our Father intended, as well as exposing them to disease and emotional devastation.

Sex-bots

For others, new technology presents "Sex-bots". Sex robots, designed to sexually satisfy without the need for relationship, commitment or any possibility of reproduction. In a lab recently, a beginning "bio-bot" had its' first Menstrual cycle.[3]

In other news

Chinese Artificial Intelligence Engineer "marries" a robot he built himself[4]

> Zheng Jiajia, 31, decided to 'marry' Yingying after failing to find a suitable human alternative. Photograph: Qiangjing Evening News.

> A Chinese artificial intelligence engineer has given up on the search for love and "married" a robot he built himself.

Zheng Jiajia, 31, decided to commit after failing to find a human spouse, his friend told Qianjiang Evening News.

Zheng had also become tired of the constant nagging from his family and pressure to get married, so he turned to a robot he built late last year and named Yingying.

After two months of "dating", he donned a black suit to "marry" her at a ceremony attended by his mother and friends at the weekend in the eastern city of Hangzhou. While not officially recognized by the authorities, the union had all the trappings of a typical Chinese wedding, with Yingying's head covered with a red cloth in accordance with local tradition.

While not widely accepted as *yet*, the way is being prepared.[5/6]
We were not created to only satisfy our cravings and longings, we were created to be in *relationship*, to be a people joined together with each other and with our Creator.
The further we grow away from each other, the further we grow away from our Creator. The further we grow away from our Creator, the further we grow away from each other. The enemy knows this and has been in process from the times of Jared to entice us away from each other and our Father God.

AI

Artificial Intelligence has become the new Weapons Race, along with Esoteric Knowledge. Such PSYOPS[7] as Mind Reading and controlling items using only the power of the mind. "Super Soldiers" implanted with the genes of animals to enable them to see at night without the use of cumbersome external equipment is a *now* goal. Enhancing our Soldiers with super strength *genetically* rather than having to use all that cumbersome equipment, is the subject of much of DARPA's (Defence Advanced Research Project Agency) budget.

DARPA Genetically Modified Humans for a Super Soldier Army By Paul A Philips

You've seen it as science-fiction on TV or in the movies, but now it's science-fact. I'm talking about the Pentagon's DARPA (Defence Advanced Research Project Agency) creation of a super soldier army with super human abilities achieved through genetic modification. Going on for some years, shrouded in secrecy, these mutants will make future wars totally different games.

The genetic modification of specific human genes will give these soldiers certain characteristics advantageous on the battlefield, giving rise to the most amazing abilities and performances.

Smarter, sharper, more focused and more physically stronger than their enemy counterparts, these soldiers will be capable of telepathy, run faster than Olympic champions, lift up record-breaking weights through the development of exoskeletons, re-grow limbs lost in *combat, possess a super-strong immune system, go for days and days without food or sleep... Then there's the emotional side. These soldiers will have the empathy genes deleted and show no mercy, while devoid of fear... Even more disturbingly, the "Human **Assisted Neutral Devices program**" involving brain controlling allows the 'joystick' remote operation of soldiers from some far away control centre.*

All this has been revealed, even in the mainstream media. In spite of the secrecy, fiction writer Simon Conway was allowed into the Pentagon's DARPA and given a guided tour... Doesn't this suggest that DARPA are well into the final stages and they want us to get use to the idea of a genetically modified super soldier army?

The type of super human characteristics that have been developed (or in the development stages) in the soldiers is indicated by funding allocations. For example, DARPA has handed out a $40 million grant to California and Pennsylvania Universities to develop **memory-controlling implants.**

It has also been revealed that DARPA awarded $9.9 million to the Institute for Preclinical Studies Texas A and M University to develop a means of surviving significant blood loss. This would overcome the normal difficulties in requiring life-saving medical treatment immediately after combat injury which is known to be difficult to give during the complications and dangers encountered on the battle field.

Another characteristic in development is having the soldiers genetically modified to hibernate throughout winter. There is a gene in squirrels that produces an enzyme in the pancreas which enables this ability. This gene can be taken from the squirrel and inserted into solders...

Summary... some serious points to consider

1. *It has to be remembered that wars are secretly manufactured for power, profit and political gain.*
So all the massive funding gone into these projects only goes into supporting false pretexts created by the *powers that be* for their own selfish means to an end...regardless of the consequences. There's never enough money for humanity but a blank cheque for war...

2. *As history has shown us any advantage created will sooner or later be matched by the enemy.*
Human genetic modification technology for military advantages shouldn't be any different and will be matched as a response by the enemy after their realization that the technology exists. Indeed, this in effect cancels out any advantages as in the historic case of the nuclear arms race with the political super powers.

3. Are we humans next?
Will the genetic modification technology extend to civilians? Rather than give us anything to our advantage, will it be used for dumbing down and control in a **scientific dictatorship?** What about those memory-controlling implants mentioned?

Consider the sinister implications: Remember the Arnold Schwarzenegger film '**Total Recall**' involving false memory implants?

4. *When it comes to genetic modification, there's always the dangers related to tinkering with life:* What about the long-term consequences and the spread of these genes over generations?

What about the potential irreversible damages as in those related to the trans-humanist agenda..? As Geoffrey Ling DARPA director at the Technologies Office said to *Agence France Presse* "It is risky..." Well, he should know! **5.** *Last but not least there are the ethical considerations...What will be the humanitarian cost?* Could this by design lead us to the road to Hell?

Thus far we are appalled at the thought of our sons and daughters being turned into a Bio-engineered Robotic Super Soldiers. But when threatened by an enemy with such capabilities, and our Government reveals we have the counter-punch, will that outrage last?

Lucifer's hidden message is, "We can do better...we can be as God." *We* can improve on our species. God was holding out on us. We've discovered secrets we can use to improve ourselves without His interference. Remembering Lucifer's Strategy to "be as God" we can see his modern-day attempt to "create" beings in *his* image, and thereby corrupt those created in God's image. We see again, through DARPA'S research the mingling of the DNA of animals with the DNA of man in order to "improve" mankind. Lucifer is once again attempting to make man in *his* image, mingling human with non-human.

He is propagating the lie, that we can have eternal life, without the Redemption provided by our Father God, through His Son Jesus.

In March of 2017 Headlines read:

Would YOU choose to live forever? Age-reversing pill that Nasa wants to give to astronauts on Mars will begin human trials within six months

- *Scientists have discovered a key signaling process in DNA repair*
- *They have used this process in the development of a drug to reverse ageing*
- *Trials on mice found that the pill repaired DNA damage after a week*
- *Nasa wants the new technology to protect its astronauts from solar radiation*

By **Harry Pettit For Mailonline**

PUBLISHED: 14:03 EDT, 23 March 2017 | UPDATED: 14:04 EDT, 23 March 2017

Scientists have made a discovery that could lead to a revolutionary drug that actually reverses ageing.

The drug could help damaged DNA to miraculously repair and even protect Nasa astronauts on Mars by protecting them from solar radiation.

A team of researchers developed the drug after discovering a key signaling process in DNA repair and cell ageing.

During trials on mice, the team found that the drug directly repaired DNA damage caused by radiation exposure or old age.

'The cells of the old mice were indistinguishable from the young mice after just one week of treatment,' said lead author Professor David Sinclair.

Human trials of the pill will begin within six months.

'This is the closest we are to a safe and effective anti-ageing drug that's perhaps only three to five years away from being on the market if the trials go well,' said Professor Sinclair.

The work has drawn the attention of Nasa, which is considering the challenge of keeping its astronauts healthy during a four-year mission to Mars.

Even on short missions, astronauts experience accelerated ageing from cosmic radiation, suffering from muscle weakness, memory loss and other symptoms when they return.

On a trip to Mars, the situation would be far worse: Five per cent of the astronauts' cells would die and their chances of cancer would approach 100 per cent.

Professor Sinclair and his colleague Dr Lindsay Wu were winners in NASA's iTech competition in December last year.

'We came in with a solution for a biological problem and it won the competition out of 300 entries,' Dr Wu said.

Cosmic radiation is not only an issue for astronauts. We're all exposed to it aboard aircraft, with a London-Singapore-Melbourne flight roughly equivalent in radiation to a chest x-ray.

In theory, the anti-ageing pill could mitigate any effects of DNA damage for frequent flyers.

The other group that could benefit from this work is survivors of childhood cancers.

Dr Wu says 96 per cent of childhood cancer survivors suffer a chronic illness by age 45, including cardiovascular disease, Type 2 diabetes, Alzheimer's disease, and cancers unrelated to the original cancer.

'All of this adds up to the fact they have accelerated ageing, which is devastating,' he said.

'It would be great to do something about that, and we believe we can with this molecule.'

The experiments in mice, from a team at the University of New South Wales, suggest a treatment for these issues is possible through a new drug.

While our cells can naturally repair DNA damage - such as damage caused by the sun - this ability declines with age.

The scientists identified that the cell signaling molecule NAD+, which is naturally present in every cell in the body, has a key role in protein interactions that control DNA repair.

Treating mice with an NAD+ 'booster' called NMN improved their cells' ability to repair DNA damage caused by radiation exposure or ageing

For the past four years, Professor Sinclair and Dr Wu have been working on making NMN into a drug substance with their companies MetroBiotech NSW and MetroBiotech International.

➡ The human trials will begin this year at Brigham and Women's Hospital, in Boston. (emphasis mine)

Only the promise of eternal life in Christ is true. The Luciferian Strategy is to promote immortality *without* Christ.

Mars:

Why the push to go to Mars? Yes, we've been told it's the most like Earth's atmosphere. But just a cursory research into the history of Wernher von Braun and hundreds of his like-minded Nazi Scientists who were brought here by our Government at the end of World War II, will reveal a much deeper reason for Mars. The Esoteric Elite have spent millions on books, movies, TV shows and earlier Radio programs introducing us to the idea of Mars. The time had come to begin de-sensitizing us to the idea. Wernher von Braun wrote a book of fiction in the 1940's about an international expedition to Mars.[7] You can download and read the manuscript from the link in the footnotes. But, for our purposes, let me just quote a couple of small excerpts from the web page promoting his book, *Project Mars*.[8]

Mankind's love affair with the planet Mars is certainly not new. "It's long been recognized that Mars is the planet in our solar system most capable of supporting life.

Until the 1970s, the existence of life on Mars remained an open question. We know today that there are no civilizations on Mars, but in 1949, when this story was written, the possibility had not yet been ruled out. In this story by Wernher von Braun, Mars has an underground civilization which is more or less on par with our own. And it is a peaceful civilization, neither bent on conquest nor paranoid about being attacked. In this story of man's first human mission to Mars, ten space ships make the journey. Upwards of 1,000 flights into Earth's orbit are required to build, supply and fuel these ten ships, and it is an international, cooperative project. In short, the undertaking is on a scale that would never happen in the real world. We tend to stick our toes in the water first, before diving in. But neither of these issues takes anything away from the story. In fact, they add to its larger-than-life-adventure quality. All other aspects of the story are very realistic. The characters think and feel like real people; the science and rocket technology are accurate and are consistent with what is being used today; the mission timeline exactly matches reality; and so on. The mission plan does not include staying to colonize or setting up a Martian base, which, again, is realistic for a first mission, von Braun went to great lengths preparing the plot for this story. The calculations and technical drawings that he developed for a Mars mission, and on which he then based this story, are included in the 65-page appendix of this book. The writing style of *Project MARS* is typical of an adventure story written in the 1940s. ... This is quite simply a story of ordinary people doing extraordinary things. Where *Project MARS* differs from most fiction of the mid-20th century is in its multiple main characters. Typical science fiction of that era involved one main character (perhaps with a side-kick) who beats the odds, saves the world, and gets the girl, pretty much all by himself. In von Braun's story there are many characters who make essential contributions, and the story will center for a time on each of them.

This may be a throwback to von Braun's stated fascination with the works of **Kurd Lasswitz**, the father of German science fiction, whose book "On Two Planets" featured a host of characters, all contributing to the plot but with individual roles. This is also consistent with how the real world works - many people working together to accomplish what must be done; each affecting and being affected by the others. It's no accident that contemporary fiction predominantly relies on this "multiple protagonist" style.

.... As much as *Project MARS* is entertainment, it can also be seen as a proposal – for international cooperation in a human mission to Mars. Von Braun clearly believed this was possible (this story takes place in the 1980s) and went to great lengths to prove as much,

both in his professional life and in his writing. When this story was written, in 1949, a manned mission to Mars was considered fantasy by the man in the street, but today very few people would deny it was possible. The reasons that we haven't done it are economic,
not technical. (**emphasis mine**)

Interesting to note Kurd Lasswitz's book presents the theory of an underworld civilization of "Martians" in the North Pole. Also noteworthy, is the heavy involvement of Kurd Lasswitz with deep Mystery Religions. Wernher von Braun, was also a consistent practioner of the Occult. Mars has been on the Occultists Radar since the days of Nimrod. In telling us of the Last Days we find in the book of Daniel 11:37-39:

> *37He will show no regard for the gods of his ancestors or for the one desired by women, nor will he regard any god, but will exalt himself above them all. 38Instead of them, he will honor a god of fortresses; a god unknown to his ancestors he will honor with gold and silver, with precious stones and costly gifts. 39He will attack the mightiest fortresses with the help of a foreign god and will greatly honor those who acknowledge him. He will make them rulers*
> *over many people and will distribute the land at a price.*

The breakdown of, "foreign god" in Hebrew is:
foreign, strange, unfamiliar
נֵכָר

foreign, unknown
לזוֹע
strange, foreign, alien
לזוֹעֲיִ
<u>foreign</u>

The word "unfamiliar" in Hebrew is still defined as "foreign, strange". I think most people would usually put the definition as "unknown"...not necessarily "foreign or strange". So, in taking the phrase "foreign god" here in Daniel 11: 39 we see the only *different* word used in the Hebrew definition is "alien".
Putting the English word "alien", as used in this verse, into a Hebrew to English translator we find the word translates as:

> Spaceman
> Hebrew:
> חייר
> English :alien, foreigner, person living in a nation where he or she is not a citizen; stranger, outsider; **extra-terrestrial, creature from outer space**

We're beginning to see why Mars is so important to the Occultist Elite.

David Flynn in his excellent, deep research work entitled, *The David Flynn Collection* notes:

> *In ancient Rome, the god Mars is said to have been worshipped in the form of two idols, one named Mars*

*Gradivus "Mars of War" and the other Mars Quirinus"
"Mars of Fortresses." ...*

*The name "Mars" itself was a Roman form of the Chaldean word
"Mar," or "Mavor" which meant "the rebel"*
David Flynn goes on further to note on the subject of the planet
Mars:

> *The revelation of an ancient civilization discovered on the
> planet bearing the rebel's name will prove that intelligent
> life, other than man, exists in the universe. The structures
> on Mars so evident in the Cydonia region will cause people
> to doubt the Bible.*
>
> *This is the strong delusion sent by God for "those dwelling
> on the earth to believe the lie." II Thess.2:11. The lie itself is
> the counterfeit messiah.*

The "Cydonian" region of Mars has stirred *much* interest in
recent years because of the "monuments" found in it's location.

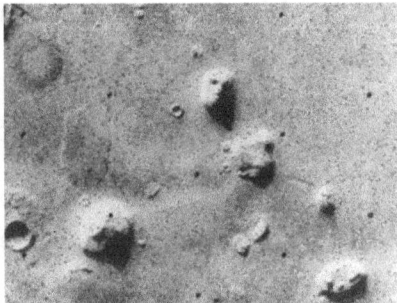

Image sent from Viking 1 from the Cydonian Region of Mars

The Cydonians of Lebanon worshipped "Baalhazor" Lord of the Fortresses. Remembering Daniel 11:38 saying he – the Anti-Christ, will "honor a god of Fortresses", we can begin to see the Luciferian Strategy to deceive, if possible, even the elect. When there is a discovery of Monuments on Mars, pointing to an earlier, much more advanced civilization. There will be a glorious return to "The Golden Age" as the Occultists and Mystery Religions like to call the days when the gods (Fallen Angels) came from heaven and interacted with mankind and taught them all the secrets the God of Creation was hiding from them.

The Golden Age

More and more in recent years, we're hearing of "the Golden Age", we're being prepared, desensitized to the terminology, like so many others, so that when we *see* it in the rise of the Anti-Christ and his alignment with the "gods" who come from "another planet," we'll be prepared to receive them.

These "gods" are coming from another *dimension* not another planet. Demons travel through walls and doors, they move from place to place in an instant, and they love to disguise themselves. In séances, they disguise themselves as dead relatives, having known the relative, they can easily imitate them. Having done DNA splicing and manipulating for centuries, they have various species of human-looking creations. They had 1200 years from the time of Jarod to the Flood of Noah to manipulate all of

Creation. Twelve hundred years ago from 2017 would take us to the year 817AD – imagine all that has transpired in that time! Imagine all that could transpire with Angelic Beings spewing the knowledge behind Creation. Those 1200 years were the years of "The Golden Age" which these entities want to return mankind to.

It is expected when these monuments on Mars are found, they may, by their depictions, cause if possible, the very elect to question the version of Creation as recorded in the Bible. Once that foundation of doubt has been established, the marvelous "miracles" shown worldwide through the wonder of Television and the Internet will cause men's hearts to be stupefied into believing a strong delusion.

Revelation tells us of coming days:

> *Revelation 13:15-16 (KJV)*
> *And he had power to give life unto the image of the beast, that the image of the beast should both speak, and cause that as many as would not worship the image of the beast should be killed.[16] And he causeth all, both small and great, rich and poor, free and bond, to receive a mark in their right hand, or in their foreheads: Revelation 14:11-12 (KJV)*
> *And the smoke of their torment ascendeth up for ever and ever: and they have no rest day nor night, who worship the beast and his image, and whosoever receiveth the mark of his name. [12] Here is the patience of the saints:*

here are they that keep the commandments of God, and the faith of Jesus.

Revelation 20:4 (KJV)

And I saw thrones, and they sat upon them, and judgment was given unto them: and I saw the souls of them that were beheaded for the witness of Jesus, and for the word of God, and which had not worshipped the beast, neither his image, neither had received his mark upon their foreheads, or in their hands; and they lived and reigned with Christ a thousand years.

But God says to those in relationship with Him in *Psalm 91:*

Whoever dwells in the shelter of the Most High will rest in the shadow of the Almighty". I will say of the Lord, "He is my refuge and my fortress, my God, in whom I trust."He is the true "God of Fortress" Surely he will save you from the fowler's snare and from the deadly pestilence. He will cover you with his feathers, and under his wings you will find refuge; his faithfulness will be your shield and rampart. You will not fear the terror of night, nor the arrow that flies by day, nor the pestilence that stalks in the darkness, nor the plague that destroys at midday. A thousand may fall at your side, ten thousand at your right hand, but it will not come near you. You will only observe with your eyes and see the punishment of the wicked. If you say, "The Lord is my refuge,"
and you make the Most High your dwelling, no harm will overtake you, no disaster will come near your tent. For he

will command his angels concerning you to guard you in all your ways; they will lift you up in their hands, so that you will not strike your foot against a stone. You will tread on the lion and the cobra; you will trample the great lion and the serpent. "Because he loves me," says the Lord, "I will rescue him; I will protect him, for he acknowledges my name. He will call on me, and I will answer him;
I will be with him in trouble, I will deliver him and honor him. With long life I will satisfy him and show him my salvation."

The Luciferian Strategy

Chapter 14

OCCUPYING

Life on planet earth isn't always easy. There are struggles and difficulties we face, no matter how strongly we believe and know our Father God through Jesus and the Power of the Holy Spirit. But following after the Truth, pressing in to know Truth, not because the way will be easier, but just to know Truth helps us to know, in the midst of the darkest of storms this life may bring, that there *is* Someone Who cares, Who strengthens, Who presses in *with* us. To be in *relationship* with our Father God is not a guarantee of ease and comfort. We don't seek to know Him because in knowing Him we will be kept from all hurt, harm and danger. We seek to know Him because He *is*. To know Him is to know Truth in our deepest being. There's a settling, a peace that passes all knowledge, wisdom, understanding. There's a rest for our very being, because we've found our Creator, our beginnings, our reason for being.

In knowing Him, there is a natural filter filtering out the enticements of the Luciferian Strategy to destroy us. Our Fathers' still, small, quiet voice of encouragement, saying, "This is the way..." filters through the loud, raucous voice of the enticement of the enemy.

If, in reading this, you've found out that you *don't* know Him, if you've found out that you don't have a *relationship* with Him, I encourage you to not wait "for a better time", we're not guaranteed tomorrow. If you've found out that you don't know Him, know that you've been introduced to Him through the pages of this work. You don't know Him intimately as yet, but you have met His intent towards you. I encourage you to receive as much as you now know of Him, receive Truth.

It's a transaction, you give Him your sin life, your sin baggage and He gives you eternal life and access to a relationship with Him. He gives you His Name and His Seal, you are then His son or daughter. Where once you were strangers, now you are adopted into His family and bear His Name. *John 3:16-21 confirms this:-*

> *For God so loved the world that he gave his one and only Son, that whoever believes in him shall not perish but have eternal life. For God did not send his Son into the world to condemn the world, but to save the world through him. Whoever believes in him is not condemned, but whoever does not believe stands condemned already because they have not believed in the name of God's one and only Son. This is the verdict: Light has come into the world, but people loved darkness instead of light because their deeds were evil. Everyone who does evil hates the light, and will not come into the light for fear that their deeds will be exposed. But whoever lives by the truth, comes into the light, so that it may be seen plainly that what they have done has been done in the sight of God.*

The Word translated "believe" actually means, to trust in, rely on, *cling* to. This verse tells us, those who do not *rely* on Jesus, have made the choice to continue walking in darkness.

Christians come under a lot of criticism for believing that the only one way to the Father is through His Son Jesus Christ. But, think about it. In our family, and yours, children became a part of our family by either being born into it or being adopted in. If, and when, a child is adopted into a family, they take on the family name. If I, a total stranger to you, declare that I am part of your family and thereby can share in, and make claim to your family wealth and provisions, you would deny me, as well you should. Another modern day analogy that helps us understand this process is email. If I *insist* I emailed you a bill for services which you did not pay, and *demand* you pay it, as well as late charges, you would ask to what email address I sent your bill. If my reply was something I had made up in my mind because it *seemed* right, you would laugh me to scorn, and no judge in the land would honor my claim against you. Why would we think the matter of Eternal Salvation would be any less stringent?

When we come to Jesus, who is the Light, and bring our darkness, asking that His Light would overtake our darkness, we then begin walking in the Light as He *is* Light. Let us allow or permit the Light of His Love, His Presence, light the path ahead for you. Psalm 119:105 says His Word is a Light unto our path. Read His Word to *know* Him and His Truth. Read His Word to learn Jesus, Who *is* the Word made flesh. Read His Word to learn Who the Holy Spirit is and all He has for you, allow Him to fill you with His Presence and give you a prayer language to search your heart and intercede for you.

> **Romans 8:26-27 (ASV)** *And in like manner the Spirit also helpeth our infirmity: for we know not how to pray as we ought; but the Spirit himself maketh intercession for us with groanings which cannot be uttered; and he that searcheth the hearts knoweth what is the mind of the Spirit, because he maketh intercession for the saints according to the will of God.*

Christians are often accused by those who don't know, of worshipping three Gods, because we worship the Father, the Son and the Holy Spirit. We worship the three as *One*, yet three distinct *in* One. A natural picture of that concept would be the humble egg. Egg white, egg yolk, egg shell – all in one egg! Three in one.

Learn of Him and you won't fear what tomorrow brings, for you'll *know* Who holds your tomorrow.

> **Romans 8: 28-31(ASV)**
> *And we know that to them that love God all things work together for good, even to them that are called according to his purpose.*

Lucifer has an End Time Plan, just as God has an End Time Plan. Lucifers' intent is to eliminate all Nations and to corrupt mankind beyond Redemption. He knows his ultimate end is eternal damnation and, knowing how it grieves the Father's heart, he wants to take as many with him as possible.

Centuries ago, God gave his Prophet Daniel a dream, recorded in the book of Daniel 2:31-45. In this dream, God reveals to Daniel what will transpire in the End Times. For our purposes, let's look at verses 43-45:

> And whereas thou sawest the iron mixed with miry clay, **they shall mingle themselves with the seed of men; but they shall not cleave one to another**, even as iron doth not mingle with clay. And in the days of those kings shall the God of heaven set up a kingdom which shall never be destroyed, nor shall the sovereignty thereof be left to another people; but it shall break in pieces and consume all these kingdoms, and it shall stand for ever. Forasmuch as thou sawest that a stone was cut out of the mountain without hands, and that it brake in pieces the iron, the brass, the clay, the silver, and the gold; the great God hath made known to the king what shall come to pass hereafter: and the dream is certain, and the interpretation thereof sure. **(emphasis mine).**

In looking at the emphasized lines, we see in verse forty-three the Father is telling us, "they **(the enemy)** shall mingle themselves with the seed of men" "*BUT* they shall not cleave one to another – even as iron does not mingle with clay." They – the Luciferian Elite - will continue to attempt to create hybrids, to manipulate mankind's DNA. According to this word, they *will* "mingle themselves with the seed of men," however, it will not accomplish what they had hoped. **(insert mine)**

This Word goes on to say, "And in the days of those kings shall the God of heaven set up a kingdom which shall *never* be destroyed...but it shall break in pieces and consume all these kingdoms, and it shall stand for ever." That is the God we serve. THAT is the Final Outcome. The outcome of the End of Times was written thousands of years ago.

Our God is a Just God. He always gives us a choice. He never violates our free-will. For that purpose, He has allowed the enemy to exist, to give mankind a choice of who to serve. Unlike Lucifer and his agents, who coerce, threaten, intimidate, entice and seduce, God holds out His promises and His Love. He displayed His Love on the Cross of Calvary for all to see and choose.

But, just as in our lives with our children, there's coming a time when He will say, "Enough." And that time is quickly coming upon us.

We've been on a journey through History. The Word of God and the inspiration of the Holy Spirit have shed light in many dark places of the Luciferian Strategy on this path.

It is not my intention to have done an exhaustive study giving all the answers. Rather, it is my heart to have shed light on areas we have been blinded to, to provoke us to continue to seek Truth. To hopefully provoke the Sons of God to *be* the Sons of God in the earth today, to *be* the Ambassadors of the Kingdom of God we're intended to be!

Now, it's for us to continue seeking the Light of Truth in coming days, for the Word says "Jesus *is* Truth,"

John 14:5-7 (ASV)

*Thomas saith unto him, Lord, we know not whither thou goest; how know we the way?⁶ Jesus saith unto him, I am the way, and **the truth**, and the life: no one cometh unto the Father, but by me. If ye had known me, ye would have known my Father also: from henceforth ye know him, and have seen him.* **(emphasis mine)**

To refuse Truth, to turn away from it, is to refuse and turn away from The One who is *all* Truth.

Never fear the Light of Truth as it continues to expose both our personal darkness and the darkness of the world around us.

Jesus *will* return in the sky with thousands of thousands of His saints and Holy Angels. Before that time, Lucifer will have his short time. Until that time, it is my prayer that we, the Representatives of Jesus, lay our lives down, whether in the peace of our pillow at night, or at the hands of one of Lucifers' agents, knowing we *fought* the Luciferian scheme against us, our families, our territories, knowing we *lived* for Truth. Knowing we *occupied* our territory until our last breath, whether that comes during a time of peace or war.

I pray the Light of the World, Jesus, will continue to shed light on our paths, as we press on to understand and dismantle the Luciferian Strategy in the times we live, so that we can,

"Occupy until He returns." Amen.

In coming years, our senses will be challenged, our "normal" will be challenged, everything we *thought* we knew will be challenged. It will no longer be enough for us to believe and hold fast to the things we were taught by others. The truth we were taught from pulpits or by our mothers or grandmothers will no longer seem to hold true. In these coming days, we will have to know the truth for ourselves. Truth *we* searched out. Because an authoritive or glamorous individual says: "*This* is the truth, *this* is how we *should* feel," does not necessarily make it true.

If we look around us we will see, and hear and know that there *is* Intelligent Design – A Creator. Jesus said: "by their fruit you will know them." Fruit is love, joy, peace, longsuffering, kindness, goodness, faithfulness, meekness, self-control. Test the fruit. Just recently, we can see the Fruit of those who thought they were well on their way to controlling the U.S. when they lost the election of 2016. Riots in the streets – not "protests" – not Free Speech being spoken – but black-clothed, weapon-wielding riots! Fruit.

Jesus *will* return in the sky with thousands of thousands of His saints and Holy Angels. Before then, Lucifer will have his short run. Until that time, it is my prayer that when our time comes to leave this earth, whether that time comes in the peace of laying our head on our pillow at night, or at the hands of one of Lucifers' agents, we will leave this earth in peace, knowing we *fought* the Luciferian scheme against us, our families, our territories, knowing we *lived* for Truth and *occupied* our territory until our last breath, whether that comes during a time of peace or a time of war.

We *can* occupy, by guarding the Truth in our lives. Keeping alert to the fruit of our actions. Forgiving those that offend us. Not living in anger, yes, we pass through anger – like a Train Station – pass *through* it, don't take up residence there! Deal with issues of your heart. *Hear* yourself and deal with you.

As a Citizen of your nation - Vote. When you vote, don't vote on personality, looks or achievement. Vote for fruit – what does the person believe, what is the fruit of their lives thus far, what are they hoping to implement in your Country? When you listen, don't listen with a filter – we tend to listen and hear an individual say something totally against reason and we immediately filter it with, "Oh no, they can't mean THAT!" LISTEN to hear. One of our recent Candidates for President espoused the belief in Sharia Law being implemented in our Nation alongside our Laws. Hearers applauded because it *looked* so "tolerant" and "inclusive" – not following the line of thinking to its Fruit – under Sharia Law Husbands can kill their daughters or wives with impunity for the *suspicion* of being with a man – not sexually – just *being* with a man. Thieves would have their hand cut off. Hanging would be restored. Women cannot vote or drive. Audiences swallowed the speeches of those who spoke with eloquence, rather than listening for the *content*. Distortions can and *will* be spoken with smooth eloquence. Truth sometimes comes in a loud, crudely spoken voice.

Be *involved* in prayer for the Politics, Church, Community you live in. If you have School boards determining what children will be learning from, run for a position or be sure to pray for good, clear-minded individuals to occupy these seats. Pray for your local Government and if you are able to, run for positions in governance, get involved. Become involved with your Church, scripture says to, "know those who labor among you," you can't know someone without spending time with them. Help where you can in your Church activities, if that's not possible, pray for those who do.

Get to know *you*. Pray, ask what your gifts and calling are. Psalm 139, among many other scriptures tells us we are not in this world by accident or the whim of our parents:

> *O Lord, You have searched me and known me. You know my sitting down and my rising up; You understand my thought afar off. You comprehend my path and my lying down, And are acquainted with all my ways. For there is not a word on my tongue, but behold, O Lord, You know it altogether. You have hedged me behind and before, and laid Your hand upon me. Such knowledge is too wonderful for me; It is high, I cannot attain it. Where can I go from Your Spirit? Or where can I flee from Your presence? If I ascend into heaven, You are there; If I make my bed in hell, behold, You are there. If I take the wings of the morning, and dwell in the uttermost parts of the sea, even there Your hand shall lead me, and Your right hand shall hold me. If I say, "Surely the darkness shall fall[a] on me," Even the night shall be light*

about me; Indeed, the darkness shall not hide from You, But the night shines as the day; The darkness and the light are both alike to You. For You formed my inward parts; You covered me in my mother's womb. I will praise You, for I am fearfully and wonderfully made; Marvelous are Your works, and that my soul knows very well. My frame was not hidden from You, when I was made in secret, and skillfully wrought in the lowest parts of the earth. Your eyes saw my substance, being yet unformed. And in Your book they all were written, the days fashioned for me, when as yet there were none of them. How precious also are Your thoughts to me, O God! How great is the sum of them! If I should count them, they would be more in number than the sand; when I awake, I am still with You. Oh, that You would slay the wicked, O God! Depart from me, therefore, you bloodthirsty men. For they speak against You wickedly; your enemies take Your name in vain.[c] Do I not hate them, O Lord, who hate You? And do I not loathe those who rise up against You? I hate them with perfect hatred; I count them my enemies. Search me, O God, and know my heart; try me, and know my anxieties; And see if there is any wicked way in me, and lead me in the way everlasting.

In the book of Acts we are told that our times and locations are not just a matter of whim if we are in relationship with Him and surrender our days to him, we are told:

> *"The God who made the world and all things in it, since He is Lord of heaven and earth, does not dwell in temples made with hands; nor is He served by human hands, as though He needed anything, since He Himself gives to all people life and breath and all things; and He made from one man every nation of mankind to live on all the face of the earth, having determined their appointed times and the boundaries of their habitation.*

If prayer is new to you, and I know that for at least some of you who read this, it will be – LEARN. There are *excellent* resources available. *Anything* written or taught by Rev. Dr. Mosy U. Madugba or his wife Chinyere Gloria Madugba will thoroughly equip you.

Be involved in the world around you. We are not *of* this world, but we *are* in this world. We are here in this time frame for a reason, to occupy this earth and, as Jesus prayed in the book of Matthew 6:9-13

> *Our Father who art in heaven, Hallowed be thy name. Thy kingdom come. **Thy will be done, as in heaven, so on earth.** Give us this day [a]our daily bread. And forgive us our debts, as we also have forgiven our debtors. And bring us not into temptation,**(testing)** but deliver us from [b]the evil one. **(emphasis and insert mine).***

In closing, I pray the Light of the World, Jesus, will continue to shed light on our paths, as we press on to *being* the Ambassadors of His Kingdom He has equipped and called us to be, and thereby manifesting the Sons of God in the earth, who understands and dismantles the Luciferian Strategy in the times we live, so that we can "Occupy until He returns",

Amen.

Footnotes

FOOTNOTES:

Chapter 1:
https://www.wordsearchbible.com/
Chapter 2:
http://www.jewishencyclopedia.com/articles/13437-seraphim
Strong's Talking Greek & Hebrew Dictionary
Abarim Publications: **www.abarim-publications.com**
Chapter 3
https://www.convert-me.com/en/convert/history_weight/
bibshekel.html?u=bibshekel&v=5%2C000

(4) Upon Ardis. Or, "in the days of Jared" (R.H. Charles, ed. and trans., The Book of Enoch [Oxford: Clarendon Press, 1893], p. 63).
Dudael (**Heb.** דּוּדָאֵל, compd. of *dud* דּוּד "kettle", "cauldron", "pot" + *El* אֵל "deity", "divinity" — lit. "cauldron of **God**") is the place of imprisonment for **Azazel** (one of the "fallen" angels), cohort of **Samyaza**. It is described in the **Book of Enoch** chapter 10 verses 4–7:
And again the Lord said to Raphael: 'Bind Azazel hand and foot, and cast him into the darkness: and make an opening in the desert, which is in Dudael, and cast him therein. And place upon him rough and jagged rocks, and cover him with darkness, and let him abide there for ever, and cover his face that he may not see light. And on the day of the great judgement he shall be cast into the fire.
Dudael is also implied to be the prison of all the fallen angels, especially the evil **Watchers**, the entrance of which is located to the east of **Jerusalem**.[1] (Streane, Annesley William. Chapman,

Arthur Thomas. (edit.) *The Book of Leviticus in the Revised Version, Volume 4*. The University Press, 1914. pg. 186.) The way this place is described, Dudael is sometimes considered as a region of the **underworld**,

comparable to **Tartarus**[2][3] or **Gehenna**.[4][5][6]

(13) Biters. More accurately, "bastards" (Charles, p. 73; Michael A. Knibb, ed. and trans., *The Ethiopic Book of Enoch* [Oxford: Clarendon Press, 1978], p. 88).

Deut. 3:11 declares that his "bedstead" (translated in some texts as "sarcophagus") of iron is "nine **cubits** in length and four cubits in width", which is 13.5 ft by 6 ft according to the standard cubit of a man. It goes on to say that at the royal city of **Rabbah** of the **Ammonites**, his giant bedstead could still be seen as a novelty at the time the narrative was written.

Chapter 7

https://en.wikipedia.org/wiki/Anno_Mundi:

Anno Mundi (**Latin** for "in the year of the world"; **Hebrew**: לבריאת העולם, "from the creation of the world"), abbreviated as AM or A.M., or Year After Creation,[1] is a **calendar era** based on the **biblical** accounts of the **creation** of the world and subsequent history. Two such calendar eras have seen notable use historically:

Arpachshad. Arpachshad,, alternatively spelled Arphaxad or Arphacsad, was one of the five sons of Shem, the eldest son of Noah (Genesis 10:22, 24; 11:10-13; 1 Chron. 1:17-18). ... He is said by Gen. 11:10 to have been born two years after the Flood, when Shem was

100.**https://en.wikipedia.org/wiki/ArpachshadArpachshad** - **Wikipedia**

http://www.marquette.edu/maqom/giants.html

[1] Josephus, *Jewish Antiquities* (LCL; tr. H.S.J. Thackeray; Cambridge: Harvard University Press/London: Heinemann, 1967) 4.33.

https://en.wikipedia.org/wiki/Giant#Names_and_tribal_ori
gins_of_giants

Josephus, *Antiquities of the Jews*, Book 5, Chapter 2, Number 3, **Antiquities of the Jews: Book 5**, Retrieved: 15 March 2013

"The Book of Enoch: The Book of Enoch: Chapter VII". *sacred-texts.com*.

Chapter 10

Megaliths from the Island of Malta

Megaliths from Peru

https://www.bibliotecapleyades.net/gigantes/esp_gigantes_
04.htm Indeed, the abundant evidence more than indicates that
there are *giants roaming Israel today.*

As there were 5,000 years ago and they also left proof of their
existence. The giants were descended from **the nefilim**, literally
the fallen ones. In ancient time, entities fell on Israel from the
heavens and later became the mortal enemies of the Hebrew
nations.

Gloryofzion.org First Fruits of Chesvan 10/22/17 Robert Heidler
https://healthresearchfunding.org/16-interesting-
gigantism-statistics/

Chapter 12
https://answersingenesis.org/bible-timeline/timeline-for-the-flood/

Chapter 13
http://www.theamericanconservative.com/2013/05/16/human-cloning-is-real-heres-what-you-need-to-*know*/
https://en.wikipedia.org/wiki/Human_cloning
https://www.thesun.co.uk/tech/3213842/robot-has-her-first-period-in-scientific-feat-which-will-bring-machines-even-closer-to-humanity/MEET THE TAMPONATOR Robot has her first period in scientific feat which will bring machines even closer to humanity Scientists recreated a vagina, uterus, cervix, liver and fallopian tubes with human tissue By Margi Murphy 30th March 2017, 12:21 pm Updated: 30th March 2017, 3:42 pm. A ROBOT has had its first period in an incredible scientific feat which brings us a step closer to creating robots in our own image. Scientists at Northwestern University used human cells to recreate a female reproductive system in a box. EVATAR could help scientists understand how medicines affect women differently from men And after switching on their lab-based creation, researchers claim that the book-sized biobot, dubbed EVATAR, had completed its first menstrual cycle. Specialists worked on each part of the reproductive system to build EVATAR; one team working on an ovary and another on the cervix. It's hoped that a number of fake organ systems could be linked up to create a "human in a dish". EVATAR is one step closer to human-styled robots It's been claimed that humans could begin to marry robots in as little as thirty years' time. But top professors including Stephen Hawking

have warned that society should be terrified of artificial intelligence and robot advances. But this new system is more likely to save lives. The Frankenstein-style creation will allow pharmaceutical companies to test new drugs on these half humans to see if they cause any nasty reactions. And in the case of EVATAR, scientists will be able to see the difference in reactions between men and women. It follows news of fleshy 'bio-bots' made of living cells which can wriggle and walk. The fleet of walking "bio-bots" are powered using muscle cells and controlled using electrical and optical pulses.

https://www.theguardian.com/world/2017/apr/04/chinese-man-marries-robot-built-himself

http://www.news.com.au/lifestyle/relationships/sex/french-woman-wants-to-marry-a-robot-as-expert-predicts-sex-robots-to-become-preferable-to-humans/news-story/fa40fc51a55564627589e80d3a527059 French woman wants to marry a robot as expert predicts sex robots to become preferable to humans

A FRENCH woman has described herself as a 'robosexual' saying real men disgust her, as experts predict we'll all be having robot sex by 2050.

ON THE surface, Lilly seems like a blushing young woman ready to marry the man of her dreams who makes her "totally happy."

Only her partner is 3D printed robot named Inmmovator who she designed herself, after realising she was attracted to "humanoid robots generally" rather than other people.

"I'm really and totally happy," she told news.com.au over email in her tentative English. "Our relationship will get better and better as technology evolves."

The "proud robosexual" said she always loved the voices of robots as a child but realised at 19 she was sexually attracted to them as well. Physical relationships with other men confirmed the matter. "I'm really and only attracted by the robots," she said. "My only two relationships with men have confirmed my love orientation, because I dislike really physical contact with human flesh."

She has since built her own dream man with open-source technology from a French company, and has lived with him for one year. They are 'engaged' and plan to marry when robot-human marriage is legalised in France.

The unconventional relationship has been accepted by family and friends but she said "some understand better than others."

She won't reveal whether they have a sexual relationship and is currently in training to become a roboticist in order to take her passion into her everyday life.

While Lilly's views will strike many as odd, it's just a sign of things to come according to David Levy.

The chess whiz and authority on **Love and Sex with Robots** said he expects human-robot marriages to become commonplace by 2050 if not before.

Speaking at the second conference on the issue held in London this week, Mr Levy told a room filled with academics and interested people that advances in artificial intelligence mean robots could become "enormously appealing" partners within the next few decades.

"The future has a habit of laughing at you. If you think love and sex with robots is not going to happen in your lifetime, I think you're wrong."

"The first human robot marriages will take place around the year 2050 or sooner but not longer," he said.
The conference explored a host of issues on the subject including everything from what robots should look like to whether they should be able to "learn" about sexual preferences and feed back information to companies behind them.

University of London Computing Professor Adrian David Cheok said he believes robots will not only become common, but preferable for many people.
"It's going to be so much easier, so much more convenient to have sex with a robot. You can have exactly what kind of sex you want. That's going to be the future. That we will have more sex with robots and the next stage is love ... we're already seeing it."

"Actual sex with humans may be like going to a concert. When you're at home you can listen to Beethoven's ninth symphony, it's good enough and once or twice a year you'll want to go the Royal Albert Hall and hear it in a concert hall.

"That may be the way sex with humans is going to be. It's going to be much more easier, much more convenient to have sex with a robot, and maybe much better because that's how you want it."
http://nypost.com/2017/08/06/sex-robot-makers-claim-lonely-customers-are-marrying-their-dolls/
Psychological operations (PSYOP) are planned operations to convey selected information and indicators to audiences to influence their emotions, motives, and objective reasoning, and ultimately the behavior of governments, organizations, groups, and individuals.

The purpose of **United States psychological operations** is to induce or reinforce behavior favorable to U.S. objectives. They are an important part of the range of diplomatic, informational, military and economic activities available to the U.S. They can be utilized during both peacetime and conflict. There are three main types: strategic, operational and tactical. Strategic PSYOP include informational activities conducted by the U.S. government agencies outside of the military arena, though many utilize Department of Defense (DOD) assets. Operational PSYOP are conducted across the range of military operations, including during peacetime, in a defined operational area to promote the effectiveness of the joint force commander's (JFC) campaigns and strategies. Tactical PSYOP are conducted in the area assigned to a tactical commander across the range of military operations to support the tactical mission against opposing forces.

PSYOP can encourage popular discontent with the opposition's leadership and by combining persuasion with a credible threat, degrade an adversary's ability to conduct or sustain military operations. They can also disrupt, confuse, and protract the adversary's decision-making process, undermining command and control.[1] When properly employed, PSYOP have the potential to save the lives of friendly or enemy forces by reducing the adversary's will to fight. By lowering the adversary's morale and then its efficiency, PSYOP can also discourage aggressive actions by creating disaffection within their ranks, ultimately leading to surrender.

The integrated employment of the core capabilities of electronic warfare, computer network operations, psychological operations, military deception, and **operations security**, in concert with specified supporting and related capabilities, to influence, disrupt, corrupt or usurp adversarial human and automated decision making while protecting our own.[2]

Between 2010 and 2014, PSYOP was renamed Military Information Support Operations (MISO), then briefly renamed PSYOP in Aug 2014, only to return to MISO shortly thereafter in 2015 **http://www.theeventchronicle.com/study/darpa-genetically-modified-super-soldiers/**

DARPA Genetically Modified Humans for a Super Soldier Army By **EDITOR** February 3, 2017 **https://www.newparadigm.ws/my-blogs/darpa-genetically-modified-humans-for-a-super-soldier-army/**

Two Planets

https://books.google.com/books?id=DSz9ngEACAAJ

Kurd Lasswitz, Erich Lasswitz - 1971 - No preview - More editions Explorers find a Martian colony at the North Pole. The Martians want to share their knowledge with earth in exchange for a supply of air and energy, but human folly leads to war. **http://www.wlym.com/archive/oakland/docs/MarsProject.pdf**

The David Flynn Collection, Defense Publishing, Crane, MO page 481

By Viking 1, NASA - Viking 1 Orbiter, image F035A72 (Viking CD-ROM Volume 10)http://photojournal.jpl.nasa.gov/catalog/PIA01141raw .imq data -

ftp://pdsimage2.wr.usgs.gov/data/.cdroms2/viking_orbiter/vo_10 10/fo35axx/fo35a72.imqraw data directly converted to .gif - http://www.solarviews.com/cap/face/035a72.htm, Public Domain, **https://commons.wikimedia.org/w/index.php?curid=218488 http://www.independent.co.uk/news/science/pet- translator-amazon-report-cats-dogs-prairie-dogs- a7854831.html**

Timeline of Genesis patriarchs

From Wikipedia, the free encyclopedia

The timeline of the **Tanakh** can be estimated using the ages given in **Genesis** and **Jubilees**. Starting with the creation of **Adam** and adding the information when his son was born, the age of his son, etc. this gives a timeline from Adam's creation to the death of **Jacob** 2255 years later (according to the **Masoretic** text, the **Septuagint** timeline is significantly longer). These timelines are used by some biblical scholars to estimate the age of the earth by counting back the number of years associated with each of the biblical patriarchs and adding the years together.

1 - **Adam** (generation 1) is created.[1]

130 - Adam and Eve receive a son, **Seth** (generation 2)

235 - **Enosh** is born (generation 3)

325 - **Kenan** is born (generation 4)

395 - **Mahalaleel** is born (generation 5)

460 - **Jared** is born (generation 6)

622 - **Enoch** is born (generation 7)

687 - **Methuselah** is born (generation 8) "Methuselah" can be translated "when he dies it comes".

874 - **Lamech** is born (generation 9)

930 - Adam dies, aged 930

987 - Enoch taken up by God (did not die [Gen5:24]), aged 365

1042 - Seth dies, aged 912

1056 - **Noah** is born (generation 10)

1140 - Enosh dies, aged 905

1235 - Kenan dies, aged 910

1290 - Mahalaleel dies, aged 895

1422 - Jared dies, aged 962

1556 - Noah has three sons: **Shem, Ham,**

and **Japheth** (generation 11)

1651 - Lamech (Noah's father) dies, aged 777

1656 - Methuselah dies **the same year as the flood comes**, aged **969**

1658 - Arpachshad is born (generation 12)

1693 - Shelah is born (generation 13)

1723 - Eber is born (generation 14)

1757 - Peleg is born (generation 15)

1787 - Reu is born (generation 16)

1819 - Serug is born (generation 17)

1849 - Nahor is born (generation 18)

1878 - Terah is born (generation 19)

1948 - **Abraham** is born (generation 20)(this should be 1946)

1958 - **Sarah**, Abrahams wife, is born

1996 - Peleg dies, aged 239 - this is the first death mentioned in the **Bible** after the **flood**

1997 - Nahor dies, aged 148

2006 - **Noah**, generation 10 after Adam, dies at the age of 950

2026 - Reu dies, aged 239

2034 - Ishmael is born (generation 21)

2048 - **Isaac** is born (also generation 21)

2049 - Serug dies, aged 230

2083 - Terah dies, aged 205

2085 - **Sarah** dies

2088 - **Isaac** is married at the age of 40, to Rebecca

2096 - Arpachshad dies, aged 438

2108 - Jacob is born, with his twin Esau (generation 22)

2123 - **Abraham** dies, aged 175

2126 - Shelah dies, aged 433

2158 - **Shem** dies, aged 600

2187 - Eber dies, aged 464
2228 - **Isaac** dies, aged 180
2238 - **Jacob** moves to Egypt at the age of 130
2255 - **Jacob** dies in **Egypt**, aged 147

FROM JOSHUA TO THE EXILE: THE PEOPLE OF ISRAEL IN THE PROMISED LAND

Audience: **Adult Individuals**   Format: **Web**Author: **The Learning Bible**

Moses led the people of Israel in the desert for forty years after they escaped from slavery in Egypt. But when the people were camped in the lowlands of Moab on the east side of the Jordan River, Moses died, and Joshua became their new leader. The promise God made more than five hundred years earlier to Abraham (**Genesis 12:1-2; 15:7-21**) and repeated to Joshua (**Joshua 1:1-8**) was about to be fulfilled. Abraham's descendants, the people of Israel, were ready to take over the land of Canaan. But this would not be easy. Other people had lived in Canaan for thousands of years. They had built walled cities and farmed the land, and they were not simply going to give their land to the people of Israel.

The people of Israel enter the Promised Land

The story of how the people of Israel conquered the people of Canaan is told in Joshua. Like the biblical books that tell about how Moses led the people (Exodus, Numbers, Deuteronomy), Joshua is full of miracles. Before the people of Israel could enter Canaan, they had to cross the Jordan River. Once again, God was with them and helped them in a miraculous way. Just as God had helped Moses by opening up the waters of the Red Sea (**Exodus 14**), so God made the waters of the Jordan River stop flowing when the priests of Israel stepped into the river (**Joshua 3:15-17**). After they crossed the river and came to Gilgal, the people made a monument using twelve rocks, one rock for each tribe of Israel. Then they set up camp there.

Here the people of Israel prepared to capture Jericho, a nearby walled city that stood on a mound along an important east-west trade route in the fertile Jordan River Valley. The conquest of Jericho is another miraculous story. After the Israelite priests and army marched around the city for seven days as the Lord had instructed, the priests blew their trumpets and the people shouted. The walls of the city fell flat and the Israelites captured the city (**Joshua 6**). From Jericho, Joshua and the people moved into other parts of Canaan, capturing other cities in battle or making agreements with the people who already lived in the land.

The Tribes of Israel and their Lands

Eventually Joshua gave different parts of the land of Canaan to each of Israel's twelve tribes (**Joshua 13—21**). These tribes were like big extended families, with the oldest male (father) serving as the center of authority. As the tribes took ownership of their pieces of land, they settled down to build towns, grow crops, and raise herds of sheep and goats. The land these tribes owned was believed to have been assigned by God, and so no one was to sell or give their property to anyone else. If that did happen, the land was to eventually be given back to the tribe God first gave it to. This would happen during the Year of the Celebration which was celebrated approximately every fifty years (**Leviticus 25:8-17,23-28**).

The tribe of Levi did not get their own land, because they were given a special task and would not be farmers or herders. The Law of Moses said they would be in charge of offering sacrifices to God (**Deuteronomy 18:1**). The other tribes were to provide these sacrifices, and the Levites were allowed to keep some of the food sacrifices for themselves. Thus, the Levites (priests from the tribe of Levi) had an important place as the religious leaders of the other tribes: they would be the priests for all Israel.

Even though the twelve tribes were scattered in different areas around Canaan, they shared a common history and followed the Law of Moses. Just before Joshua died, he called all the tribes together for a meeting at Shechem. He challenged them to remain faithful to God and never to worship other gods (**Joshua 24:14-24**). The people promised to remain faithful, and Joshua set up a stone as a witness to their promises (**Joshua 24:25-27**).

Judges are chosen to rule the people of Israel

After Joshua died, the tribes of Israel continued to fight against the Canaanites (**Judges 1**), but they did not drive out all the people who had lived in the land. In addition, the tribes of Israel were also surrounded by other peoples who were not friendly.

At this time, the Israelites began to forget the promises they had made to the Lord while Joshua was still alive. Some of them worshiped the Canaanite gods, Baal and Astarte, as well as idols of other gods from nearby lands (see the article called **The Ancient World: Peoples, Powers, and Politics**). The Lord was so angry that he let the surrounding nations raid Israel's lands and steal their crops and possessions (**Judges 2:6-15**).

When the people cried out for help, God felt sorry for them. Help came from special leaders known as judges. The judges sometimes settled legal cases (see **Judges 4:4-5**), but most of them were more well known as military leaders chosen by God to lead the Israelites in battle against their enemies. The lives of these judges are described in Judges chapters 3—16 (see also the **Introduction to Judges**).

Samuel: Prophet, Priest, and Leader

Near the end of the period of the judges, a boy named Samuel was born to Hannah and Elkanah (**1 Samuel 1**). They took him to

Shiloh, where he was dedicated to the Lord by the priest Eli. Samuel stayed with Eli in Shiloh and helped Eli serve the Lord. While Samuel was still very young (**1 Samuel 3**), the Lord chose him to be his special servant and he grew up to be the Lord's prophet (**1 Samuel 3:19; 4:1; 7:3-5**). Samuel also served as a priest (**1 Samuel 7:9-10**)and was a leader in Israel all his life (**1 Samuel 7:15**). Because his time as Israel's leader immediately followed the period of judges, he is sometimes called the last of Israel's judges.

Kings and Kingdoms
When Samuel was getting old, the leaders of Israel's tribes asked him to choose a king to rule over them, because all the lands around them were ruled by kings. Samuel did not really like this idea. He believed that a king would not treat the people well (**1 Samuel 8:9-18**), and he thought that the people's request for a king showed their lack of trust in the Lord as their leader (**1 Samuel 10:17-19**). But when Samuel prayed about the situation, the Lord told him to go ahead and give the people a king (**1 Samuel 8:1-22**). This was a major change in the history of the Israelite people. For a long time they had been a loosely connected group of tribes with one God but separate leaders. Now, they were about to become a single nation made up of tribes united not only by one God, but also under a king.
The people of ancient Israel were ruled by kings from the time of Saul (about 1030 to 1010 B.C.) and David (1010 to 970 B.C.) to the reign of Zedekiah (597 to 587 B.C.). Some of the kings were strong rulers who remained faithful to God. But other kings actually led the people away from worshiping God, made bad agreements with Israel's enemies, and treated the people cruelly and unfairly. The

history of the kings is told in 1 and 2 samuel, 1 and 2 kings, and is retold in 1 and 2 chronicles.

Saul: Israel's First King

The period of the kings is divided into two main parts. The first part is known as the time of the United Israelite Kingdom, when there was just one king for all of the Israelite people and tribes. Samuel chose Saul to be the first king of Israel 1 **Samuel 9,10** and he was accepted by the tribal leaders because of his courage and military abilities 1 **Samuel 11**. He ruled for about twenty years and did much to bring the tribes together and to defeat some of Israel's enemies. But Saul was also a troubled man who was unfaithful to God at times.

David Becomes Israel's King

While Saul was still king the Lord told Samuel to go to Bethlehem to find the next king. This turned out to be David, the youngest son of Jesse (1 **Samuel 16:1-13**). David soon entered Saul's court as a special servant who played the harp to console the troubled king (1 **Samuel 16:14-23**). Another account of David's life shows him to be an amazingly brave soldier who trusted in the Lord. David killed the giant Philistine Goliath (1 **Samuel 17:1-54**) and impressed the king so much that Saul made him a high officer in the army (1 **Samuel 18:5**). Eventually, the king became suspicious of David and jealous of his military successes. Saul tried several times to have David killed, but was never successful. Eventually, Saul committed suicide after being injured in battle against the Philistines (1 **Samuel 31:1-13**).

After Saul's death, there was a short period when the people of Israel were divided between loyalty to Saul's only living son,

Ishbosheth, and to David, the powerful military leader. David became king of the people of Judah at Hebron (**2 Samuel 2:4**), and then king of all of Israel after the murder of Saul's son (**2 Samuel 5:1-3**). He then conquered the Jebusite city Jerusalem and made it the capital of the United Israelite Kingdom (**2 Samuel 5:6-12**). He put the sacred chest (see the mini-articles called The Sacred Chest and The Sacred Tent on the hilltop where the temple would later be built (**2 Samuel 6:1-19**). The prophet Nathan told David that God would dwell in the great temple in Jerusalem some day. But he said that David's son would build it, not David (**2 Samuel 7:1-17**).

One of greatest things David did was to defeat the Philistines in battle and take control of all the land east of the Jordan River and north of Damascus in Syria as far as the Euphrates River (**2 Samuel 8**). Psalms and the books of the prophets describe David as a model king who had a close relationship with God. In many ways, he became a symbol of new life for God's people and of God's rule in the world (**2 Samuel 23:5; Psalm 89:3-4; Isaiah 9:1-7; Jeremiah 33:14-26; Micah 5:2-5**). However, David also had his faults (see, for example, **2 Samuel 11—12** and the article called **David**).

Solomon: Israel's Wisest King

David's son, Solomon, became king after David died and ruled from about 970 to 931 B.C. Solomon was known as a wise man (**1 Kings 2:9; 3:12, 28; 4:29-34**), and he was in charge of building Israel's first temple in Jerusalem (**1 Kings 5-8**). He expanded his father David's kingdom, built an enormous palace (**1 Kings 7:1-12**) and many fortresses, established store cities, and made Israel a very rich country (**1 Kings 4: 20-28**). But in doing this he married foreign wives and allowed them to set up shrines and monuments to other gods (1 **Kings 11:1-13**), things which were certainly not pleasing to the Lord.

The Kingdom Is Divided

When Solomon died around 922 B.C., his son Rehoboam became king. Shortly after that, the ten northern tribes rebelled against the king and formed their own kingdom. This period of Israel's history became known as the Divided Kingdom.

The tribes of Judah and Benjamin in the south became known as the kingdom of Judah (or the southern kingdom). The rest of the tribes to the north formed the kingdom of Israel (or the northern kingdom). See the map called The Kingdoms of Israel and Judah. Each kingdom had its own king. In Judah, the kings continued to be descendants of King David, but in Israel the tribal and military leaders had to fight to become king. Sometimes a family would reign for a period of years, only to be defeated by an opponent who then ruled for a time.

The capital of Judah was still Jerusalem where the people of Judah continued to worship the Lord in the temple. But in Israel, King Jeroboam I made a shrine in Bethel so that people could offer sacrifices there instead of going to the temple in Jerusalem (1 **Kings 12:25-33**). Later, Samaria became the capital city of Israel (1 **Kings 16:24-29**).

Israel: The Northern Kingdom

In the northern kingdom of Israel, some rulers allowed the people to worship idols such as the Canaanite god Baal. This practice was condemned by a number of the prophets who preached in Israel during this time. For example, the prophet Elijah spoke out against King Ahab and his wife Queen Jezebel, who openly encouraged the worship of Baal and supported Baal's prophets (see 1 **Kings 18:1—19:18**).

The practice of allowing the people to worship other gods led to Israel's downfall. They fought civil wars with Judah and battled with neighbors like Syria and Moab. Eventually, the Assyrians invaded Israel and attacked the capital city of Samaria. In 722 B.C. the city was conquered and many of the Israelites were captured and taken away to Assyria as prisoners. Others stayed in the area, lived with, and sometimes married the people the Assyrians brought in to settle the land. The northern kingdom of Israel never regained its power as a nation.

Judah: The Southern Kingdom

Meanwhile, Judah in the south had its own problems. Though many of its kings, such as Hezekiah and especially Josiah, were faithful to God and followed the teachings of the Law of Moses (**2 Kings 18:1-8**), other kings, like Manasseh, did things to make the Lord angry (**2 Kings 21:1-18**). Eventually Judah could no longer hold out against the attacks of its powerful neighbors. The kingdom of Babylon finally invaded and destroyed Jerusalem and its temple in 587 B.C. Many of the people of Judah were taken to Babylon as prisoners. During the next fifty years this group of Israelites remained in Babylon and could not return to their own land. This period of time is known as "the exile." (See article called **Exile**). To learn about how the people of Israel were allowed to return to their homeland, see the article called **After the Exile: God's People Return to Judea**.

References *(in Alphabetical Order)*:

Randy DeMain, *Nephilim Resurgence,* Kingdom   Revelation Ministries, Inc, Autin, TX, 2012

Randy DeMain, *The Nephilim Agenda,* Kingdom   Revelation Ministries, Inc, Autin, TX, 2010

Richard J. Dewhurst, *The Ancient Giants Who Ruled America,* 2014, Dear & Company, Rochester, Vermont, 05767

David Flynn, *The David Flynn Collection,* Defense Publishing, Crane, MO 65633

Mark A. Flynn, *Forbidden Secrets of the Labyrinth,* 2014Defender, Crane, MO

Derek P. Gilbert, *The Great Inception,* 2017, Defender, Crane, MO 65633

Dr. Michael S. Heiser, *Reversing Hermon,* 2017, Defender, Crane, MO 65633

Thomas Horn and Cris Putnam, *On the Path of the Immortals,* 2015, Defender Publishing Co., Crane, MO. 65633

Thomas Horn and Josh Peck, *Abaddon Ascending,* 2016, Defender Publishing Co., Crane, MO. 65633

Thomas Horn, *Zenith 2016,* 2016, Defender Publishing Co., Crane, MO. 65633

Ken Johnson, *Fallen Angels,* 2013, Biblefacts Ministries, Biblefacts.org

Ken Johnson, *Ancient Post Flood History*

Ken Johnson, *Ancient Book of Enoch,* 2012

Ken Johnson, *Ancient Book of Jasher,* 2008

Dr. Michael Lake, *The Shinar Directive,* Defender, Crane, MO

Heather Lynn, PHD, *Land of the Watchers,* 2015, The Midnight Crescent Publishing Co., Cleveland, OH

Rev. Dr. Mosy U. Madugba, *Apostolic Leadership,* Spiritual Life Publishing, Port Harcourt, Nigeria
#3 Babbe Street, D/Line, PO Box 7960
Port Harcourt, Nigeria

Rev. Dr. Mosy U. Madugba, *Four Levels of Spiritual Warfare,*
Spiritual Life Publishing, Port Harcourt, Nigeria
#3 Babbe Street, D/Line, PO Box 7960
Port Harcourt, Nigeria

Rev. Dr. Mosy U. Madugba, *Prayer Power,*
Spiritual Life Publishing, Port Harcourt, Nigeria

#3 Babbe Street, D/Line, PO Box 7960
Port Harcourt, Nigeria

Rev. Dr. Mosy U. Madugba, *Elders at the Gate,*
Spiritual Life Publishing, Port Harcourt, Nigeria
#3 Babbe Street, D/Line, PO Box 7960
Port Harcourt, Nigeria

Rev. Dr. Mosy U. Madugba, *Understanding the Ministry of Apostolic Women,*
Spiritual Life Publishing, Port Harcourt, Nigeria
#3 Babbe Street, D/Line, PO Box 7960
Port Harcourt, Nigeria

Rev. Dr. Mosy U. Madugba, *God's Unbeatable Army,*
Spiritual Life Publishing, Port Harcourt, Nigeria
#3 Babbe Street, D/Line, PO Box 7960
Port Harcourt, Nigeria

Rev. Mrs. Chinyere Gloria Madugba, *Brokenness,*
Spiritual Life Publishing, Port Harcourt, Nigeria
#3 Babbe Street, D/Line, PO Box 7960
Port Harcourt, Nigeria

Rev. Mrs. Chinyere Gloria Madugba, *The Jael Company,*
Spiritual Life Publishing, Port Harcourt, Nigeria
#3 Babbe Street, D/Line, PO Box 7960, Port Harcourt, Nigeria

L.A.Marzulli, *On the Trail of the Nephilim, Vol. 1,* 2013,

Spiral of Life Publishing,

L.A.Marzulli, *On the Trail of the Nephilim, Vol. II,* 2014,
        Spiral of Life Publishing,

Kimberly Wilson (Johnson) , *Preparing for Battle,*
Amazon.com

Skywatchtv.com
Youtube.com/skywatchtv

Footnotes

www.ingramcontent.com/pod-product-compliance
Lightning Source LLC
Chambersburg PA
CBHW051958090426
42741CB00008B/1450